the
FOOTBALL
BOOK *of*
WHY

(AND WHO, WHAT, WHERE, WHEN & HOW)

Also by the Author

All the Moves I Had: A Football Life (with Raymond Berry)

America's Football Factory: Western Pennsylvania's Cradle of Quarterbacks from Johnny Unitas to Joe Montana

Remembering the Greatest Coaches and Games of the NFL Glory Years: An Inside Look at the Golden Age of Football

Remembering the Stars of the NFL Glory Years: An Inside Look at the Golden Age of Football

You're the Ref: 174 Scenarios to Test Your Football Knowledge

the FOOTBALL BOOK *of* WHY

(AND WHO, WHAT, WHERE, WHEN & HOW)

THE ANSWERS TO QUESTIONS
YOU'VE ALWAYS WONDERED ABOUT
AMERICA'S MOST POPULAR GAME

WAYNE STEWART

LYONS
PRESS

Essex, Connecticut

To my family: wife Nancy, sons Sean and Scott, daughters-in-law Rachel and Katie, and my grandson Nathan.

Also to my cousin Dale Stewart, a rugged fullback out of Carnegie Tech who was as comfortable with his artist's palette as he was with the pigskin.

An imprint of Globe Pequot, the trade division of
The Rowman & Littlefield Publishing Group, Inc.
4501 Forbes Blvd., Ste. 200
Lanham, MD 20706
www.rowman.com

Distributed by NATIONAL BOOK NETWORK

Library of Congress Cataloging-in-Publication Data available

ISBN 978-1-4930-6857-9 (paper : alk. paper)
ISBN 978-1-4930-6858-6 (electronic)

♾™ The paper used in this publication meets the minimum requirements of American National Standard for Information Sciences—Permanence of Paper for Printed Library Materials, ANSI/NISO Z39.48-1992.

Contents

Introduction

Any beginning journalist knows that every story he works on should, when applicable and not irrelevant to the story, contain the answers to the questions readers are most curious about. These all-important questions are known as the five Ws and an H—who, what, when, where, why, and how.

To gain a full and rich understanding of football, those questions are, of course, vital. Fans, even ardent ones, may know all of their favorite players' statistics and all of the major records set by the game's greats, yet lack knowledge about some other points.

This book provides a slew of questions and in-depth answers concerning the rules, records, and history of the NFL, and much more. From the early days of football to the popular game seen today, there's a good chance that this book answers questions every fan has pondered. Whether the topic is quarterbacks or coaches, famous "firsts" or memorable moments, if a who, what, when, where, why, or how question is on your mind, this is the book for you.

While the primary emphasis here is on pro football, some questions pertain to the college game. Also, unless otherwise noted, all of the statistics, records, and feats mentioned in the book are through the 2021 season.

The game of football has undertaken quite an evolutionary ride, one deserving of study. So, sit back, relax, and get ready to be entertained, informed, and even surprised by the facts which follow.

CHAPTER ONE

THE ORIGINS AND EARLY DAYS OF AMERICAN FOOTBALL FROM ITS BIRTH THROUGH 1922

As touched upon in the introduction, modern fans often are lacking when it comes to their knowledge of the roots of football. How did football gets its start? What are its roots? Where did those roots first take hold?

If you happen to be one of those fans who isn't savvy about those early days, *and* you find such ancient history to be boring, you can either skim through this chapter or skip it entirely. However, if you skip the chapter, you'll miss out on some odd, fascinating, and entertaining items such as the following: some rules which now seem bizarre at best; a champion that wasn't, by later standards, really the champ; and a title game which was played on a field which measured just 60 yards long.

Just as baseball can trace its beginnings back to England and a game called rounders, football evolved from the game of rugby, a sport which also originated in England.

In the United States, the first college game of "soccer football" took place in 1869 when Rutgers and Princeton squared off on November 6. That contest employed "modified London Football Associated rules." Over the next seven years rugby became quite popular, surpassing soccer in popularity, especially with major colleges in the East.

From there, the next logical evolutionary step was for modern football to modify rugby, resulting in football becoming its own sport with its own rules, strategies, and intricacies.

However, there are many more facets which went into the early days of football. This chapter explores those roots, including the pioneers of the sport, the early rules of the game, and more.

ALL SPORTS REQUIRE CLEAR-CUT RULES, EVEN THOUGH THE EARLIEST ONES MAY HAVE VARIED A BIT DEPENDING UPON SOME FACTORS SUCH AS GEOGRAPHY. ALSO, MANY OF THOSE RULES BECAME OUTDATED, EVEN OBSOLETE, OVER THE YEARS. NEVERTHELESS, A KEY QUESTION IS THIS: WHO WROTE UP THE FIRST RULES FOR AMERICAN FOOTBALL AND WHEN?

Walter Camp, now known as the father of American football, created many rules and changes to the sport in its early stages. In 1876, rules were drawn up at the Massasoit convention. Over a stretch of 15 years, Camp continued to meet with various athletic directors of colleges to refine the game's rules.

Before Camp, college ball was not unlike what one source called "the medieval European sport of mob football." In fact, Camp was a star running back at Yale, a school which had once banned the brutal sport (when Camp was an infant). Furthermore, before Camp, every college team played under their own set of rules.

WALTER CAMP, THE "FATHER OF AMERICAN FOOTBALL" (Library of Congress)

Among Camp's innovations were reducing the number of players on the field from 15 to 11, adding "measuring lines to the field," and having a "static line of scrimmage." At one point he also came up with a rule which stated the team on offense had to gain 5 yards in three tries or surrender the football. That, of course, led to the four downs being allotted to advance the ball 10 yards scenario we now have. Camp invented the quarterback position and the concept of calling signals on offense. It is stated that by 1892, "he had created the game we now know as football."

ONE OF THE MOST BASIC PARTS OF FOOTBALL IS, OF COURSE, THE TACKLE. HOW HAS THE DEFINITION OF WHAT CONSTITUTES A TACKLE, THAT IS TO SAY, AT WHAT POINT IS A BALL-CARRIER'S RUN FINISHED AND THE PLAY IS DEAD, CHANGED OVER THE YEARS?

At one time, a player's run wasn't blown dead until his forward progress was fully stopped. It wasn't enough to be, say, on the ground when a defender was making some contact with the man carrying the football. It almost seemed as if ball-carriers were sometimes unsure if they were down or not, and they would fiercely scratch for every extra yard until a whistle blew. In fact, runners who were slammed to the turf could, at times, get back up and legally run again.

Joe Walton, a defensive end/receiver from 1957 to 1963, said that it appeared that if the ball-carrier was knocked down, but not *pinned* down, the play could continue. Piling on a runner was almost a requirement to stop his progress. Walton said, "Guys used to be able to get back up and run after they were knocked down. Guys were getting hurt."

Research done by Jon Kendle of the Pro Football Hall of Fame revealed that the 1921 *Spalding Official Football Guide* contained a rule regarding when a play was considered to be through. It stated that, among other things, a player with the ball would be declared to be down when he is out of bounds, has his forward progress stopped, "or when any portion of his person except his hands or feet, touch the ground *while he is in the grasp of an opponent*" [italics added].

Kendle added, "By 1932 there was a provision to the rule and 'while he is in the grasp of an opponent' was taken out [for college football]. Since the NFL created their own rulebook in 1933, that change did not apply to them and they continued to use the 'while in the grasp of an opponent' phrase. In 1948 [the NFL] added 'irrespective of the grasp being broken.'

"It wasn't until 1956 that the NFL declared that the ball is dead when 'a runner . . . is contacted by a defensive player and he touches the ground with any part of his body except his hands or feet.'"

WHO WAS THE FIRST PROFESSIONAL FOOTBALL PLAYER?

William "Pudge" Heffelfinger. Back in 1892, athletic clubs from various areas of the United States were heavily into the relatively young sport. One heated rivalry was between the Allegheny Athletic Association and the Pittsburgh Athletic Club. To gain an edge, the Allegheny group convinced an All-America guard out of Yale, Heffelfinger, to play for them against the Pittsburgh Athletic Club on November 12—persuading him with a paycheck for $500. This was at a time when a pound of bacon cost 13 cents, a gallon of milk delivered to one's door ran about a quarter, and a five-pound bag of sugar set a person back just 28 cents.

Allegheny must have felt he was well worth the money when they walked away with a win after their new star scooped up a Pittsburgh fumble and romped 35 yards for a touchdown. Final score, 4–0.

WHY WASN'T THAT FINAL SCORE 6–0?

Beginning in 1893, a touchdown was worth four points and a "goal after touchdown" was good for two points. In 1897, a rule change awarded five points for touchdowns and one point for the extra-point conversion. It wasn't until 1912 that scoring a touchdown earned a team six points.

For the record, the two-point conversion was first introduced to American football in 1958, when the NCAA came up with that idea. High schools went along with the two-point play in 1969, and the Canadian Football League joined in (1975). The NFL would not adopt the play until 1974, although the American Football League (AFL) had the option to go for two since its inception in 1960.

In addition to the vacillating number of points awarded for touchdowns, things were, by our way of thinking, strange way back in football's Dark Ages. For instance, until 1889, after a player crossed the goal line, he had to literally touch the ball down, to the ground. From then on, merely possessing the football while reaching the goal line was sufficient.

IF HEFFELFINGER WAS WITH THE ALLEGHENY ATHLETIC ASSOCIATION TEAM FOR ONLY ONE GAME, WHO IS CONSIDERED TO BE THE FIRST MAN TO SIGN A PRO FOOTBALL CONTRACT? WHEN?

It is believed that a halfback named Grant Dibert was the first player to be under contract to a team. Having lost to Allegheny, which had the help of Heffelfinger, the Pittsburgh club placed Dibert under contract for their entire 1893 season.

Now, the first player to "openly turn pro" is said to be John Brallier, a 16-year-old quarterback who received $10 plus expenses for his services in a 1895 game his Latrobe YMCA team played against the Jeannette Athletic Club (two western Pennsylvania teams). Remember, though, there were at least seven other men who accepted money to play football. That list, as mentioned, is headed by Heffelfinger, with Ben "Sport" Donnelly of Allegheny following closely behind, playing in one game a week after Heffelfinger for $250.

WHEN DID TEAMS TRULY TURN PRO BY HAVING THEIR ROSTER FILLED OUT BY MEN WHO WERE ALL GETTING PAID TO PLAY FOOTBALL?

One year after Brallier turned pro, in 1896, the Allegheny Athletic Association again made history by fielding a team composed entirely of pro players, doing so for their season, albeit a season which ran just two games.

In 1897, the Latrobe Athletic football team was completely made up of pros throughout their roster for a full season—a truly *full* one, not a mere two games or so.

WHY WAS IT THE CASE THAT SOME AMATEUR FOOTBALL PLAYERS SAW SUNLIGHT THROUGHOUT THE WINTER MONTHS ONLY ON GAME DAYS?

There are tales of men who labored in coal mines in Pennsylvania who reported to work deep beneath the earth's surface before sunrise, and whose work day ended after sunset—doing this six days a week. Then, on their only day off, Sunday, they spent some of their precious daylight hours on the football field taking part in another, but more enjoyable, dangerous endeavor.

WHAT WAS THE EQUIPMENT LIKE FOR PLAYERS DURING THE EARLY DAYS OF FOOTBALL? DID THEIR GEAR PROVIDE MUCH PROTECTION?

Protection? That's a joke. Back in the era of baggy pants with no protective pads at all, players were exposed, vulnerable to injuries galore. During the days when football was a sort of spin on rugby, starting in the late 1860s, the helmet was perhaps the biggest joke of all. Actually, football began without the use of any protective headgear as evidenced in the first college football game ever, a Princeton versus Rutgers 1869 clash. This was a pure invitation for concussions and serious, enduring brain damage.

The origin of the helmet is unknown even though some say James Naismith, the creator of the game of basketball, came up with the concept. Others claim a US Naval Academy player named Joseph M. Reeves asked an Annapolis shoemaker to devise a leather helmet for him to use in the 1893 Army-Navy game.

Therefore, it is believed that the first use of helmets in a game did take place in that contest, but the Reeves helmet was one merely "made out of leather strips or mole skin fused together."

The earliest of helmets were so pliable, and therefore virtually useless as effective protection, they could be folded up and placed into a player's pocket. They didn't even cover a player's entire head, nor did they have an ear flap. Helmets finally got

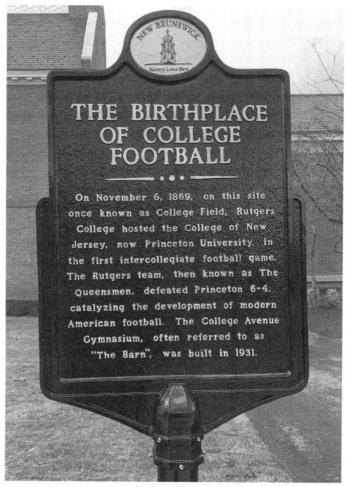

NEW BRUNSWICK

History Lives Here

THE BIRTHPLACE OF COLLEGE FOOTBALL

• • •

On November 6, 1869, on this site once known as College Field, Rutgers College hosted the College of New Jersey, now Princeton University, in the first intercollegiate football game. The Rutgers team, then known as The Queensmen, defeated Princeton 6-4, catalyzing the development of modern American football. The College Avenue Gymnasium, often referred to as "The Barn", was built in 1931.

A PLAQUE COMMEMORATING THE FIRST COLLEGE FOOTBALL GAME BETWEEN RUTGERS AND PRINCETON IN 1869
(Marylandstater via Wikimedia Commons)

substantially stronger in the 1940s and 1950s when they were constructed with padded plastic.

Regardless, college rules makers didn't make wearing helmets compulsory until 1943. As for the NFL, there was a Chicago Bears end named Dick Plasman who played without a helmet as late as 1940. That made him the last man ever to play a pro game without a helmet—it may also have made him the bravest or the most foolish player in NFL annals.

Of course, before effective facemasks were added to helmets, players often took a shot to the mouth, nose, and cheeks—with many blows being intentionally thrown. No wonder: There wasn't even a penalty for facemasking until late in the 1950s.

The first shoulder pads, which came about in 1877, are believed to have been made of wool and leather and were actually "sewn into the competitor's jerseys." Not long after 1900 came the introduction of shoulder pads which were pulled down over one's head and attached at players' chests. Even as late as 1990, shoulder pads tended to be quite large and cumbersome, but they now are smaller yet strong.

A few other equipment notes: It wasn't until right around 1920 that players began wearing leather padding. The 1930s saw more foam pads with decent facemasks being added to some players' helmets. As time went on, the single- and double-bar facemasks and other such alterations came along. The decade of the 1940s saw the influx of leather shoulder pads, chest pads, and chinstraps. Face shields for helmets didn't come about until 1998. Today's helmets look almost aerodynamically designed.

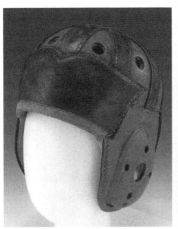

A MICHIGAN WOLVERINES FOOTBALL HELMET CIRCA 1930S (LEFT) AND ITS MODERN-DAY EQUIVALENT (Wikimedia Commons)

HOW HAVE THE FACEMASKS EVOLVED OVER FOOTBALL'S HISTORY?

Early facemasks had a single bar covering a small portion of players' faces. Former college fullback Dale Stewart said: "That was a laugh. We had that single bar in college in the late 1950s and into 1960. We [Carnegie Tech] were punting, and I'm standing out on a wing ready to block a big defensive end. He came up with a forearm, caught that bar and pushed it right up, and that bar was like nothing. There was no stability on that single bar. I knew I had a broken nose. I'd have been better off if the bar wasn't there. It was no good from the beginning. Whoever came up with that idea must have never played football."

Then came the double bar which was a *little* better. Later came other variations such as the cage-type mask, covering much of the face. Players, such as receivers, who rely upon their vision more than linemen (who also want the added protection of larger facemasks) don't want a mask which would obscure their all-important vision to any degree.

Players nowadays wouldn't think of wearing a helmet sans facemask, but that wasn't the case long ago. Joe Walton, who spent seven seasons in the NFL with New York and Washington, never wore a facemask until his senior year at Pitt, 1956. "It was just a small bar across the face. Then I went to the Redskins and Kelly Miller was the equipment manager. When I went to get my helmet, he asked me what size facemask I wanted. I told him, 'I don't really need one. I wore one at Pitt and didn't like it.' He said, 'Well, I'm just advising you, you ought to learn to use one, but if you want to wait, it's all right with me.'

"We played the Los Angeles Rams in our first preseason game and guess what happened? A player broke my nose. The next week I went into Kelly and I said, 'Give me one of those things.'"

WHAT WAS ONE OF FOOTBALL'S EARLIEST FORMATIONS WHICH SOON PROVED TO BE ONE OF ITS MOST DANGEROUS?

The perilous "flying wedge" formation was a tactic which was soon outlawed. The wedge, which resembled a V-formation of geese in flight, was unveiled in an 1892 Harvard versus Yale game and it soon spread, even to the point of being used on some plays from scrimmage. It took only two years before the flying wedge was banned.

It originated on kickoffs with players locking themselves together and/or running shoulder-to-shoulder, forming a plow-like wedge and acting just like a plow, barreling into would be tacklers at full or nearly full speed while serving as a human shield for the ball-carrier. This formation often led to some very nasty injuries.

Even now, there is a 15-yard (or half the distance to the goal) penalty in the NFL for forming an illegal wedge.

WHY WAS THERE AN OUTCRY DEMANDING THAT FOOTBALL BE BANNED IN THE EARLY 20TH CENTURY?

In 1905, a reported 18 high school and college football players died due to the "unnecessary roughness" of the sport. In addition, according to the *Washington Post*, at least 45 died from 1900 to October of 1905. Most fatalities came from broken necks, broken backs, concussions, and internal injuries.

So, in 1905, the president of the United States, Teddy Roosevelt, himself a big football fan, held a meeting with coaches and several athletic advisers. Rather than ban football, Roosevelt had a goal to improve the sport, "especially by reducing the element of brutality in play." Previously, he had said, "I believe in rough games and in rough, manly sports. I do not feel any particular sympathy for the person who gets battered about a good deal so long as it is not fatal." By 1905, it was evident that football was, in fact, causing many a fatality.

The death of one player, a Union College halfback named Harold Moore, really stirred things up. He died after being kicked in the head while going for a tackle, and somehow *that* grabbed the nation's attention. Clearly, football's image was tarnished—one newspaper ran an editorial cartoon which portrayed the Grim Reaper sitting on a goalpost. Columbia, Northwestern, and Duke even suspended their football programs.

The result of Roosevelt's actions and the glaring publicity over the many injuries and deaths caused by football led to rule changes for the 1906 season. One major new rule permitted forward passes and added the wide receiver position to the game, opening up the field which helped eliminate so many tight scrums. Another rule, which also helped avoid massive pile-ups, stated play must stop when any player fell on the ball.

WHY WASN'T THE PASSING GAME A BIG PART OF FOOTBALL AT FIRST?

As mentioned in the previous item, the forward pass wasn't even permitted at first. Not only that, but once it was allowed, early rules involving the forward pass actually discouraged its use, so this weapon didn't take off right away. For example, an incomplete pass cost the team on offense to the tune of a 15-yard penalty, and a pass that fell to earth without even being touched resulted in a turnover. By the way, before the forward pass was legalized, one rather common practice was to use short, lateral "passes."

The first legal forward pass took place on September 6, 1906, when Bradbury Robinson of Saint Louis University let the football fly. Unfortunately, it was off target, untouched by his intended receiver so, by rule, it was as bad as throwing an interception.

However, in 1907, Pop Warner's Carlisle Indian Industrial School made an impact with their passing game when they took on the undefeated and *unscored upon* University of Pennsylvania. That day Warner, unafraid of trying something new (and famous for devising and/or using trick plays) enjoyed watching his players complete 8-of-16 passes, with one thrown by Jim Thorpe. Experts agree that more than any other coach, Warner and what he did in 1907 deserves credit for creating the modern passing game.

Actually, even before that eye-opener, Carlisle had been a juggernaut. They won their first six games by a composite score of 148–11. Still, the win over Penn seemed to garner the most attention. And it was a one-sided victory: Carlisle won, 26–6, and racked up 402 yards to 76 for the Quakers.

Another early contest which gained much attention for a successful passing game was Notre Dame's stunning 35–13 win over Army on November 1, 1913. Gus Dorais went 14-for-17, amassing 243 yards with some of his completions coming on throws to Knute Rockne. Incidentally, by the time that game was held, penalties for incompletions were no longer in effect. Passing was here to stay.

Meanwhile, the Pro Football Hall of Fame website states, "The first authenticated pass completion in a pro game came on October 27, 1906, when George (Peggy) Parratt of Massillon threw a completion to Dan (Bullet) Riley in a victory over a combined Benwood-Moundsville team."

WHY IS A FOOTBALL REFERRED TO AS A PIGSKIN?

The obvious answer is incorrect—the football was never made out of the skin of pigs—Porky, Miss Piggy, and Babe were safe. One source states that the first footballs were made of inflated animal bladders filled in with material such as straw. The bladders, usually those of pigs, were then wrapped up in leather. The FanBuzz website noted that the phrase "throwing the ole pigskin" is a lot more appealing than saying "throwing the ole pig's bladder."

The first football made of leather and which came with lacing was introduced in 1887 by Al Spalding, a man who once played Major League Baseball. In fact, he led the majors in wins in each of his six full seasons, twice winning more than 50 games, and winning nearly 80 percent of all of his decisions, including one year when he won 91.5 percent of his decisions (54-5). Obviously a big name in sports, he later made his fortune as a sporting goods magnate.

WHEN DID TEAMS FIRST GO INTO HUDDLES?

The practice of sharing information in a huddle, especially the next play a team was calling, dates all the way back to 1894. Gallaudet University, a school for the deaf, was led by quarterback Paul Hubbard, who was worried that an opposing team might be able to figure out what play he was going to run because he was signing the information openly to his team. It was only natural then that on the days when his team met the Pennsylvania Deaf School and the New York Deaf School, he combated any sign stealing by having his team circle around him.

Hubbard went on to become an instructor at the Kansas School for the Deaf. There, in 1899, he again employed the huddle. Before long, that method of play-calling permeated the Midwest and an innovation took hold and spread.

WHY IS A FOOTBALL FIELD, TO THIS DAY, SOMETIMES CALLED A GRIDIRON?

The word *gridiron*, by the way, dates back to the 14th century when it was used to describe a grid made of iron which was used to cook food over an open fire.

Although the appearance of any football field today has little if any true resemblance to a grid or a gridiron, football fields were originally laid out in a checkerboard pattern with horizontal and vertical lines intersecting each other all over the field.

HOW DID THE TERMS FOR MEMBERS OF THE BACKFIELD ORIGINATE?

Before the T-formation became widespread, teams basically tended to utilize four offensive players situated in the backfield. The quarterback stationed himself about "one-fourth" of the way behind his line, two halfbacks started out next to each other and "halfway" back from the line of scrimmage, while the fullback was set the farthest back of the four players.

WHAT WERE THE NAMES OF SOME OF THE FIRST PRO FOOTBALL FRANCHISES, WAY BACK IN 1922?

A look back at the very first pro teams ever reveals some not so familiar names. Actually, three of the NFL's charter members are still in existence—the Chicago Cardinals in their Arizona Cardinals embodiment, the Chicago Bears who started out as the Decatur Staleys, and the Green Bay Packers, the oldest team never to change its venue.

The Canton Bulldogs were the 1922 champions, and other teams included the Toledo Maroons, the Rock Island Independents, and the Racine Legion. Dayton's team was known as the Triangles, while another Ohio team was the Akron Pros. Milwaukee's nickname was the Badgers, and the Oorang team was called the Indians. Rounding out the league: Louisville Brecks, Minneapolis Marines, Rochester Jeffersons, Columbus Panhandles, Hammond Pros, and the Evansville Crimson Giants. Two teams played 12 games that year, two played 11, and Evansville lasted just three contests.

WHICH TEAM IS THE OLDEST PRO FOOTBALL TEAM IN CONTINUING OPERATION, AND WHEN WAS IT FOUNDED?

The team in question, which began simply as a neighborhood team on the South Side of Chicago, was called the Morgan Athletic Club. It was founded a long, long time ago in 1899. Name changes followed and the team later became known as the Normals, then they became the Racine Cardinals, and the Chicago Cardinals. Fans of more recent years may recall the team's 28 seasons spent in St. Louis as the Cardinals. Next came the change of venue as the team became the Phoenix Cardinals. Since 1994, the team has gone under the name of the Arizona Cardinals. Therefore, it can honestly be said that the Cardinals franchise has spanned parts of three centuries.

Their history is a rich one as they won two championships and churned out such stars as their all-time leaders—Ottis Anderson for rushing, and Larry Fitzgerald for receiving—as well as Hall of Famers in tight end Jackie Smith and defensive backs Larry Wilson, Dan Dierdorf, Roger Wehrli, and Aeneas Williams.

WHAT WAS THE FIRST TEAM TO WIN THE NFL'S CHAMPIONSHIP—AND WHICH TEAM WON WHAT MIGHT BE CALLED THE FIRST "TRUE" CHAMPIONSHIP, BY WINNING THEIR TITLE ON THE FIELD?

This is a tricky one because there were times when the (pre-NFL) American Pro Football Association (APFA) teams played some of their contests against teams which were not part of that official league. For the 1920 season's title, the Akron Pros were awarded the championship at an APFA meeting which wasn't held until April 30, 1921. The league's champ was determined based on win-loss percentage, and all ties were ignored in the calculations.

Akron was undefeated in 1920, but were saddled with three unsatisfying ties, giving them a perfect winning percentage at 8-0-3. Two teams, the Decatur Staleys (10-1-2 in their first of only two years of existence before moving to Chicago as the Bears) and the 9-1 Buffalo All-Americans bitterly disputed Akron's title, but to no avail.

The first actual title game was held on December 17, 1933, when George Halas's Chicago Bears, 10-2-1 on the season, defeated the 11-3 New York Giants at Wrigley Field by a narrow

23–21 margin. This contest was set up when, in July of that year, the NFL was split into two divisions (called conferences after 1949). The two division winners were to meet thereafter to determine the champions, and that setup stayed through the 1966 season when the two conferences were divided into a total of four divisions.

WHAT MADE JIM THORPE SO SPECIAL?

As King Gustaf V of Sweden placed gold medals around Thorpe's neck during the 1912 Olympics held in Stockholm, awarded to him for winning the grueling pentathlon and decathlon events, he stated, "You, sir, are the greatest athlete in the world." Thorpe's point total in the decathlon was 8,412, almost a staggering 700 points better than the second-place finisher, setting a record he held until 1948.

An article by Sally Jenkins for the *Smithsonian Magazine* described Thorpe as being "a ripped 185 pounds with a 42-inch chest, 32-inch waist and 24-inch thighs." Jenkins quoted Olympic historian Bill Mallon as saying pictures of Thorpe show him to look "almost modern. He's cut. He doesn't look soft like the other guys did back then." He took that physique and his athletic skills to the football fields and became a legend.

Side note: The International Olympic Committee stripped Thorpe of his medals when they learned he had participated in the Olympics while not, by their definition, an amateur—he had played professional baseball in the minors in 1909 and 1910. By today's rules, this fantastic Native American would have been eligible to claim the medals. In 1982, the medals were restored to him posthumously.

While he wasn't a star in baseball, it should be noted that few aspiring athletes are good enough to enjoy even a sip of baseball's proverbial big-league cup of coffee, let alone last six

JIM THORPE IN 1915 (Wikimedia Commons)

seasons, which Thorpe did from 1913 to 1919, mainly with the New York Giants—not to mention his Olympic and football feats. Still, Thorpe did help prove the Ted Williams theory which contends hitting a baseball is the single most difficult feat in sports—Thorpe's lifetime batting average was only .252.

He did make major-league history, though, when he took part in a game which featured both starting pitchers throwing no-hitters through nine innings. On May 2, 1917, Thorpe was an outfielder for the Cincinnati Reds, who faced the New York Giants and their pitcher Hippo Vaughn. After Vaughn and Reds hurler Fred Toney had breezed through nine innings of no-hit ball, the Reds finally broke up the no-hitter on a single by Larry Kopf. He eventually reached third base and scored the game's only run when Thorpe tapped a short groundball in front of the plate and, with his speed, legged it out for what turned out to be the game-winning hit.

He joined the ranks of pro football in 1915, becoming a two-sport player, with the pre-NFL Canton Bulldogs. Listed at 6'1" and a solid 202 pounds, he could do it all—and for just $250 per game at first. He had the ability to pass, catch passes, punt, and kick field goals. He was a one-man Punt, Pass, and Kick event.

On defense his tackles were described as bone jarring. He once said, "When old Jim hits them, they rattle."

In 1950, the Associated Press (AP), looking back over five decades, updated King Gustav's appraisal of Thorpe, naming him the greatest athlete of the first half of the century. Sadly, this legend died in poverty.

CHAPTER TWO

THE NFL FROM 1922 THROUGH 1999

In a way, the sort of unofficial birth of the NFL came during a meeting of the owners of 11 football franchises held in Canton, Ohio, on September 17, 1920. They formalized a league, then named the American Professional Football Association (APFA). The historic meeting was not held in a posh setting—instead it was hosted by the Canton Bulldogs owner, Ralph Hay, in, of all places, the showroom of his Hupmobile auto dealership. Jim Thorpe was selected to head the association as its president. Two years later at another owners' meeting in Cleveland, a constitution was drawn up and the team owners officially changed the name of their group to the National Football League.

Other important decisions were still to come, such as the establishment of a new rule which would ban the use of players who were still active in the college ranks. But this meeting remains another important historical football moment, marking the origin of the NFL.

This chapter covers the range from the 1922 season through the 1999 season, a long and remarkably glorious era, studded with superlative stars, feats, and memories.

WHO IS CONSIDERED TO BE THE LAST MAN TO PLAY BOTH WAYS IN AN NFL CONTEST?

Many point to Chuck Bednarik, aka Concrete Charlie, aka 60 Minute Man, as being the last man to regularly play both offense and defense. Some seasons he was the center for Philadelphia Eagles, and for many years he manned a linebacker spot, dishing out crushing blows to opponents who dared enter his territory.

The versatile Hall of Famer stood 6'3" and tipped the scales at 233 pounds; and he was as tough as a filled-to-the-rim keg of rusty nails. Over his 14-year career he missed just three games, and he earned All-Pro honors at both the center and linebacker positions.

In the 1960 NFL championship game versus Vince Lombardi's Green Bay Packers, the 35-year-old Bednarik was on the field for 58 minutes and 30 seconds, missing only 1:30 during kickoffs. The Bethlehem, Pennsylvania, native helped hand Lombardi what would be his only postseason loss ever. After losing this one to the Eagles, Lombardi went 9-0 in playoff action.

When Roy Green broke in with the St. Louis Cardinals in 1979, he was perceived by his Cardinals coach Jim Hanifan as a defensive back. That changed in 1981 when Green was given the opportunity to also play on offense as a receiver. Shortly after, on the first pass he caught in the NFL he gained 60 yards. One week later he recorded his first touchdown on a 58-yard reception and,

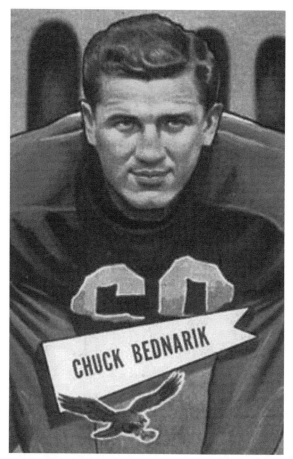

CHUCK BEDNARIK (Bowman Football Card via Wikimedia Commons)

a bit later, he picked off a Joe Theismann pass. In doing this, he became the first man to score on a pass and pick a pass off in the same contest since 1957.

Green was named to two Pro Bowl games, and he was a two-time All-Pro as well. Both of his berths on the All-Pro team were earned for his playing as a wide receiver in 1983, the year his 14 receptions led the NFL, and 1984, the year he chalked up a personal high and league leading total of 1,555 yards via catches. He retired with more catches as well as the most receiving yards and the most touchdowns on receptions than any other Cardinals player.

He also was gifted enough to return at least some punts and kickoffs in eight of his 14 seasons spent mainly with the Cardinals franchise in St. Louis and Phoenix. He only scored one touchdown on kickoff returns, but it was a doozy. It came in his rookie season of 1979, and its distance of 106 yards led the NFL that year.

In a college game in 1978, Green returned a kickoff 90 yards for a score, ran back a punt 65 yards for a touchdown, returned an interception 40 yards for yet another score, and tossed in a blocked field goal for his Henderson State University team. Absolute versatility.

However, as Bednarik himself once pointed out, Green fell short of being a pure "both ways" player. When a sportswriter mentioned Green to Bednarik, pointing out how he was a receiver who would play in the Cardinals' "umbrella defense," Bednarik snarled, "Don't give me that b.s. You've got to play every down."

More recently, New England's Troy Brown saw some action at both the wide receiver position and at cornerback, and he returned punts and some kickoffs during his 1993–2007 career. He even retired as the team leader in receptions. In 2004, he was on the receiving end of 17 passes and, due to a bit of a desperate situation with the Patriots defense, he also saw action in the secondary, picking off three passes. Once he even filled in during an emergency as a quarterback. However, experts do not consider him a pure both ways player, a 60-minute man like Bednarik.

Likewise, some defensive players will be briefly inserted into games for, say, a play or two, lined up as a receiver or situated in the backfield like a running back, often when their team is in the red zone. A few examples of these "two-way" players are William "The Refrigerator" Perry, J. J. Watt, Adoree' Jackson, and Mike Vrabel; and a few examples of offensive players who have seen at least some action on the other side of the ball include Rob Gronkowski and Julian Edelman.

WHY WAS FOOTBALL PERMITTED TO CONTINUE TO BE PLAYED DURING THE YEARS OF WORLD WAR II?

Just as US president Franklin Roosevelt urged Major League Baseball to play throughout World War II for the good of the country, football also played on.

Baseball's quality suffered greatly with stars such as Stan Musial, Ted Williams, Hank Greenberg, and Bob Feller no longer on the scene. In all, more than 500 big leaguers served in the armed services during World War II.

The caliber of baseball was so bad while the war raged on that one of the worst teams ever, the St. Louis Browns, won their only pennant back then—one trip to the World Series over their many years of miserable existence from 1902 until 1954 when the franchise was transported to Baltimore to become the Orioles. In 1945, the final year before the war ended, they even played a one-armed outfielder by the name of Pete Gray.

The same paucity of skilled players held true in the NFL. Talent was depleted with stars such as Sid Luckman (who took part in the D-Day invasion), Chuck Bednarik (a B-24 waist gunner), Gino Marchetti (Battle of the Bulge), Ernie Nevers (who reached the rank of major in the US Marine Corps serving in the Pacific Theater of Operations), and Whizzer White (a lieutenant commander in the Office of Naval Intelligence) in faraway places.

JACK LUMMUS PLAYED FOR THE NEW YORK GIANTS AND WAS POSTHUMOUSLY AWARDED THE CONGRESSIONAL MEDAL OF HONOR FOR VALOR ON IWO JIMA. (USMC History Division via Wikimedia Commons)

Some players avoided seeing action because they were placed in Special Services and spent much of their time doing, what else, playing football. Still, 638 players, a large chunk of the NFL's talent pool, was in the Armed Forces during World War II. Remember, back then there were just 10 teams in the league, so rosters obviously were hit hard. Furthermore, 19 or 20 players (sources vary) were killed in action. Two players earned the Congressional Medal of Honor, Jack Lummus of the New York Giants and Maurice Britt of the Detroit Lions.

The NFL couldn't count on a bunch of college kids filling the ranks as many of them also wound up serving their country. Desperate owners such as George Halas sought any semblance of ability they could unearth. Halas held tryouts in an effort to find warm bodies, or as he put it, to sign "anyone who could run around the field twice." Despite the growing sense of urgency, the NFL still was unyielding in their unwritten agreement not to sign Black players.

Former NFL player Joe Walton, who hails from Beaver Falls, Pennsylvania, the same hometown of Joe Namath, pointed out an oddity caused by the small NFL talent pool. "The Steelers and the Eagles even combined their teams," he said. "That gave birth to a 1943 team." That blended team had the unlikely, unofficial nickname of the Steagles—really! The following season the Steelers this time combined forces with the Chicago Cardinals to become the "Car-Pitts." They played like the pits, going 0-10 and being outscored 328 to 108.

World War II also caused a change in the rulebook about substitution of players. Previously, the rules concerning when and how many players could enter games were quite complex. By and large, players would therefore play both ways. The new rules led to teams having both an offensive and a defensive unit.

HOW AND WHEN DID THE PRO FOOTBALL HALL OF FAME GET ITS START?

Compared to Major League Baseball's first-ever sports Hall, the NFL's Hall of Fame is an infant. The first class of Cooperstown Hall of Famers came in 1936, but the Pro Football Hall of Fame's birth, the planning stages, only dates back to 1960. Groundbreaking was held in August of 1962, and its doors didn't open until September 7, 1963, fittingly in Canton, Ohio, the place where the American Professional Football Association was founded in 1920, and the

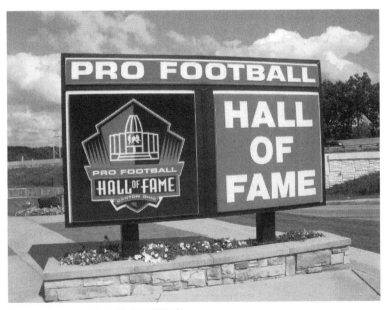

THE PRO FOOTBALL HALL OF FAME OPENED ITS DOORS IN 1963. (Wikimedia Commons)

city which had been the home of the legendary powerhouse Canton Bulldogs.

The Hall honored 17 charter members; a few of those honored were: Jim Thorpe, Red Grange, Ernie Nevers, Bronko Nagurski, Sammy Baugh, Harold "Red" Grange, Don Hutson, and George Halas.

As of this writing, the Chicago Bears have the most Hall of Famers with 30 men enshrined, ranging from charter members Halas, Nagurski, and Grange to Brian Urlacher (Class of 2018) and 2020 inductees Jim Covert and Ed Sprinkle. If other men who played a small portion of their careers with the Bears are tossed into the mix, the number of Bears in the Hall rises to 36, but that's a bit of a stretch. For example, Bobby Layne was a Bear in just his rookie season, starting one game, and Orlando Pace spent a dozen years with St. Louis before playing his final season, 2009, with the Bears.

Interestingly, only one honoree never spent as much as one play in the NFL. That man was Billy Shaw, a guard who was with the Buffalo Bills from 1961 through 1969, *before* the AFL-NFL merger, making for a great trivia question.

WHEN DID WEIGHTLIFTING BECOME A BIG PART OF THE TRAINING REGIMEN IN THE NFL?

Things were quite primitive in college football, and even in the NFL in its earlier decades. Linebacker Myron Pottios played in three Pro Bowl games over a career which spanned 1961 through 1973, mostly with the Rams. His older brother Ray played for Penn State where he was a teammate of Rosey Grier and Lenny Moore. Myron said Ray introduced him to a crude form of training long before their college days.

With no sophisticated systems in place, Myron said, "Ray would improvise. To get the effect of lifting weights to build muscles, he would push me around in a car to build up his legs, to gain lower body strength. For squats, he would put me on his shoulders and do the squats. We didn't have the weights. I continued that training when I got to high school.

"Weights weren't mandatory in the NFL until 1969—that's the first time I ever saw any connected with a football [training facility] on site. The only reason we [the Los Angeles Rams] got the weights was our coach George Allen traded for Bob Brown who played for the Philadelphia Eagles as an offensive tackle, and he loved to lift weights.

"Our first universal gym was 1969 and it wasn't mandatory that we lift weights, it was just that when Brown came over he wanted a place to lift weights."

Pottios added that during his college days at Notre Dame, "there was a weight room that you could go to which was open, but to all the students. So once I went to Notre Dame I didn't have to push cars," he quipped.

College fullback Dale Stewart remembered his days at a smaller school than Notre Dame. "We didn't have a weight room at Carnegie Tech, and they didn't promote lifting—I never heard a word about lifting weights. There was nothing formal about what we did. Our locker room was just a bunch of lockers they put in the boiler room. Everything was substandard. Back then it was totally different from what goes on today, even in high school."

Stewart also pointed out that during both practices and games "there was no water on the field for players. They gave us salt pills thinking that solved our problems." Instead of fixing dehydration issues, salt pills actually could lead to dehydration while increasing the risk of players suffering from heat illness, a true peril for summer training sessions and scrimmages as well as early-season games when the autumn sun was still blazing in many parts of the country.

WHY DO NFL EXPANSION TEAMS USUALLY EXPERIENCE MANY GROWING PAINS, AND FOR MANY YEARS?

The system the NFL used to supply new teams with players was often far from generous. In his autobiography, *All the Moves I Had*, Raymond Berry wrote about how "the league granted the Cowboys a franchise, but the 'generous' NFL owners gave them absolutely nothing. They gave them the bottom three players off the rosters of all 12 teams.

"So when Tom Landry started in 1960 [as the Dallas head coach], he basically had no talent whatsoever. The pre-expansion teams didn't want anybody to compete with them, but they wanted the money they'd get for the new franchise. They took the money and gave the Cowboys nothing.

"Landry not only had to overcome adversity, he started by inheriting a situation with a totally empty arsenal. It also took a lot of years going through the draft to finally put a team together that could compete. In their first season they went 0-11-1 and they never topped five wins until 1965."

A more recent example of a team which anguished through severe growing pains was the new rendition of the Browns. The city of Cleveland was without an NFL franchise from 1996 until 1999. Browns team owner Art Modell had bolted from Cleveland, taking his entire squad to Baltimore to become the Ravens. The new version of the Browns that came to Cleveland in 1999 had a composite record of 5-27 over its first two years of existence.

By 2002, only three of the 37 players the Browns acquired in their expansion draft were still on their roster, and all three were relegated to playing on special teams. The new version of the Browns finished in last place in six of their first eight seasons, and it took them until 2020 to make just their second postseason appearance since their origin.

There are many factors to account for such futility over so long a period of time, but being an expansion team is never easy. The Tampa Bay Buccaneers lost all 14 of their games in their inaugural season, 1976, and went 2-12 the following year—they even lost the first 26 games they ever played, establishing the longest losing streak since the AFL and NFL merged in 1970. Their winless season set a new NFL record even though later teams were worse. The Detroit Lions of 2008 and the Browns of 2017—who had also been horrendous at 1-15 in 2016—both went winless over a 16-game season. But, to Tampa Bay's credit, they righted their ship and won their conference by their fourth season.

New Orleans Saints teams were so bad that their win total over their first six seasons was a meager 20. They didn't win more than five games until 1978, 11 years after their birth. Quarterback Archie Manning, coming off tremendous years at Ole Miss, led them to that 7-9 season, but two years later his Saints (aka the Aints) went 1-15.

Manning, whose real first name is Elisha, wound up with a record of 35-91-3 in games he started for New Orleans. At Ole Miss, his school went 22-10-1 over his three years as a starter.

In 1970, the Saints' running game was so pathetic, fullback Tony Baker led the team in rushing with 337 yards. Furthermore, the Saints scored just 17 touchdowns all year long and their not-so-hot defense gave up 40 TDs. No wonder they won just twice that season.

WHICH NEW TEAMS BUCKED CONVENTION AND HAD SUCCESS RELATIVELY QUICKLY?

The 1971 Miami Dolphins were a shining exception to the rule; they made it to the Super Bowl in just their sixth season. Furthermore, they'd go undefeated the next season at 17-0 to win it all.

Then, in 1996, two expansion teams, the Carolina Panthers and the Jacksonville Jaguars, made it all the way to the conference championship contest in their second season of existence. This meant Jacksonville went from a 4-12 season to tip things off in 1995, to a conference title game in Year Two. Meanwhile, Carolina, a winner of 12 games in 1996, improved so quickly, they made it to the Super Bowl by 2003, their ninth season.

Historically speaking, the first modern expansion team to make it to a Super Bowl was the Minnesota Vikings of Bud Grant. The Vikings deserve more credit than they get for their success around and into the 1970s, as they made the playoffs in 10 of 11 years from 1968 through, including four trips to the Super Bowl.

WHICH TWO TEAMS HAVE LOST FOUR SUPER BOWLS WITHOUT A VICTORY?

The Buffalo Bills lost four consecutive Super Bowls from 1991 to 1994. The Minnesota Vikings lost Super Bowls in 1970, 1974, 1975, and 1977.

While the 11 players who were on the Vikings roster for all four of the losses deeply regret coming away empty handed, placekicker Fred Cox said, "It doesn't bother me as it always bothers Minnesota fans. When you're playing and you know that you gave it everything you had, if you lost, you lost. There is nothing you can do about it. You only have to live with yourself, and I know that we worked hard and we gave it our best shot."

Putting a positive spin on the issue, and proud of what the Vikings did achieve, Cox added, "I got four NFC Championship rings. I have four children and they all have one. I've told them many times, 'They're yours to do whatever you want with them—you can keep them, you can sell them.' Needless to say, they kept them."

As for the Bills, Hall of Fame quarterback Jim Kelly took them to postseason play in eight years and advanced to the Super Bowl in half of those seasons. In fact, he was the first quarterback ever to guide a team to the Super Bowl in four consecutive seasons. Unfortunately, the Bills lost each of those title games.

Kelly once pointed out that his peers such as John Elway and Dan Marino said they were "amazed at how we were able to do that." That's quite a compliment, but fickle fans focus only on the defeats, not realizing most teams would be overjoyed to have such a run of success. Somehow, like Cox, Kelly took the losses rather philosophically—at least on the surface. His high school coach, Terry Henry, noted, "I know the losses in the Super Bowl killed him, but on the outside you wouldn't know it."

ACCORDING TO THE BLEACHER REPORT WEBSITE, WHO ARE THE TOP THREE "SHUTDOWN CORNERBACKS" OF ALL TIME?

Their number three choice was Steeler great Mel Blount (1970–1983, all with Pittsburgh), who played with the fire and mentality of a linebacker. His 57 interceptions still rank number 13 all-time, a testament to his skill. Bleacher Report credits him with popularizing the style of play cornerbacks utilized in the 1970s, noting his bumping of receivers at the line of scrimmage, bumping that man yet again off the line, and even thumping "him when he tries to make his cut." If that wasn't enough, Blount would "bludgeon him the moment the ball arrives." He was responsible for "the so-called Mel Blount Rule" which banned making contact with receivers beyond a given point. Pro Bowl linebacker Mike Lucci stated that before the rule change, "In the old days you could knock the shit out of receivers all over the field. Today you can't touch a receiver after he goes five yards."

The number two spot went to Mike Haynes of the Oakland Raiders (after he had been cast off by the New England Patriots). No longer permitted to chuck receivers, he "combined speed, size, fluidity, technique and reliability to become the perfect cornerback to combat '80s offenses." Opposing quarterbacks tended to focus on the side of the field opposite Haynes, who constantly covered his man like Linus's security blanket.

The selection for the top man among the three men listed who all became Hall of Famers was Deion Sanders. He played for five teams from 1989 through 2005, while missing three seasons when he went into his first retirement at the age of 33. He never led the NFL in interceptions—his high-water mark was seven—because other teams knew throwing his way could be futile or disastrous. However, in 1994 when he was with the San Francisco 49ers, he led the league in yardage coming on the return of interceptions with 303, and his three returns for touchdowns also ranked number one in the NFL. While he had a reputation for being gun shy about making contact and for being a weak tackler when he did bring (or try to bring) someone down, he clearly is still considered a big-time shutdown cornerback.

WHAT IS THE CURRENT HEIGHT OF THE UPRIGHTS, AND WHEN AND WHY WERE THEY LENGTHENED FROM THEIR PREVIOUS HEIGHT?

In 1965, the Baltimore Colts were one win away from advancing to the NFL championship game, but they first had to get by the Green Bay Packers. The Colts had a three-point lead with just under two minutes to go in regulation when Don Chandler lined up for a 22-yard field goal attempt.

His kick approached, then sailed higher than, one of the uprights. The kick was then signaled "good" by referee Jim Tunney who thought the ball would have gone between the uprights (barely) had they extended higher in the sky. Tunney was forced to picture an imaginary line extending above where the post ended in order to make his call. The Colts were positive the kick was wide, outside of the right upright. Even Chandler's body language showed he thought he had missed. Seconds after getting the kick off, he swiveled his head away from the goalposts in an "Aww man," look of disgust; or, as one writer put it, he looked "much the way a golfer looks when he misses a short putt."

The game went into overtime and the Packers prevailed, winning on another Chandler kick. They then moved on to capture the title against the Cleveland Browns, 23–12, with nine points coming on Chandler field goals.

Due to this controversial call, the two uprights were changed from their 10-foot height to 20 feet. The change is sometimes referred to as "Baltimore extensions." Some 31 years later, Chandler himself confessed, "When I looked up, the ball was definitely outside the post."

Another change came about due to the infamous call: Instead of just one referee stationed under the goalpost on kicks, two officials were positioned by the goalposts. The NFL also ruled that, starting in 1967, all goalposts had to be bright gold in color.

The height of the uprights now is 35 feet, a change brought about after another questionable kick. In 2012 New England lost a 31–30 decision to the Baltimore Ravens on a Justin Turner kick which soared higher than the top of an upright. For the record, the width of the crossbar is 18 feet and six inches, and it sits 10 feet above the ground. So, actually, the tops of the uprights loom 45 feet above the turf.

WHAT IS THE PENALTY FOR A DEFENSIVE PLAYER ATTEMPTING TO BLOCK FIELD GOALS BY LEAPING UPON THE BACKS OF TEAMMATES?

At one time, a player, say a sleek defensive back, could legally take a few quick strides from, say, a yard or so behind the line of scrimmage and hurl himself onto the back of a teammate to gain height, a move sometimes called "climbing the ladder," to try to block a kick. Nowadays, this is a leverage penalty, one which is considered to be unsportsmanlike conduct. It carries a 15-yard penalty plus an automatic first down. Another strategy once legally employed was for one player to lift another one to, again, elevate the man trying to block a field goal.

In addition to those now illegal tactics, a rule came into effect for the 2018 season banning another clever trick. There were some players, very athletic, acrobatic ones, who could time the snap perfectly and who would then jump over an offensive lineman to swiftly get to the kicker.

That move became controversial during the 2017 season when Bobby Wagner, a Seattle Seahawks linebacker, used the ploy to block a field goal attempt by Arizona's Chandler Catanzaro. The game ended in a 6–6 tie. The Cardinals head coach, Bruce Arians, was quite vocal, protesting what he considered to be a bush league trick. His main issue, though, was the "safety for the center, who must keep his head down before snapping the ball and likely won't see a defender leaping over him."

A Seattle teammate of Catanzaro, safety Kam Chancellor, was another man who gained recognition for his ability to employ the move.

WHO WAS THE FIRST PLAYER IN THE NFL WHO WEIGHED 300 OR MORE POUNDS? WHICH PLAYERS HAVE EXCEEDED 400 POUNDS?

The first 300-pounder was 10-year veteran Roger Brown, a defensive tackle for the Detroit Lions and later with the Los Angeles Rams. He was listed at 6'5" and 300 pounds on the nose over his career, which ran from 1960 through 1969. He may have been a behemoth then, but he was not a lumbering oaf. He was selected to play in six Pro Bowl games. Still, he was regarded by many back then as a bit of an oddity—not a sideshow freak, but a sight to see for sure. In today's game he'd fit right in. The average offensive lineman from just a handful of years ago checked in at almost exactly the same height and weight as Brown at 6'5" and 312 pounds.

Brown has nothing on more recent players. According to the FanBuzz website, the three heaviest players to ever suit up (and in a huge "suit") in the NFL are Aaron Gibson, Terrell Brown, and Nate Newton. All three of these giants topped the 400-pound strata at one time or another.

The FanBuzz countdown: the third heaviest man, guard/tackle Newton, weighed "just" 401 pounds and gained most of his fame with the Dallas Cowboys. Another big man of the Newton era of the mid-1980s and into the 1990s was William

CAM NEWTON IN 2014. BY THE STANDARDS OF THE 1960S, HE WOULD BE CONSIDERED A LARGER-THAN-AVERAGE OFFENSIVE LINEMAN.

"The Refrigerator" Perry (382 pounds at his peak), so Newton, by extension, was given the larger nickname of "The Kitchen." The 6'3" Newton won three Super Bowl titles and was a six-time Pro Bowl honoree.

The next heaviest player was offensive tackle Terrell Brown who weighed 403 pounds at one point, and who stood at a looming 6'10". The top spot belongs to Gibson who at his peak reportedly carried 410 pounds on his 6'6" frame. He is said to have gone as high as 440 in high school.

Bonus item: The tallest man to ever play in the NFL was defensive tackle Richard Sligh who was outfitted in a uniform that very well may have been specially made as he stood exactly 7 feet tall (and weighed exactly 300 pounds). That placed this veteran of one season, 1967 with the Oakland Raiders, three inches taller than a man who came along in 1974—a man who became known as "Too Tall," Ed Jones of Dallas Cowboy fame.

Final note—in 1960, the average offensive lineman stood 6'3" and weighed 251 pounds. A 2015 article by Cork Gaines pointed out that quarterback Cam Newton, at 6'5" and 250 pounds, is larger than most of the offensive linemen from the 1960s.

HOW DID PLAYERS IN EARLIER ERAS SOMETIMES DISREGARD THEIR OWN COACHES' WISHES?

The most obvious answer, and perhaps the most frequent infraction, is breaking curfew. There's a famous story about Green Bay Packer head coach Vince Lombardi fining receiver Max McGee $250 for a curfew violation. That didn't change McGee's ways, so the next time he tried to sneak back to the team's training camp late, he was caught and this time slapped with a $500 fine plus the admonishment, "And the next time it'll be $1,000." Lombardi then added, "And if you find anything worth $1,000, let me know and I may go with you."

Of course, breaking curfew often meant breaking another unwritten rule: Don't play while hungover. One player said, "Hell, yes, we played with hangovers. That made us play mean."

Violating other rules such as reporting late for meetings was another way players have been known to tick their coaches off. Lombardi was seen by his players as a tough disciplinarian, but also a benevolent patriarch at times. He detested players coming late to his meetings. Then again, he was wise enough to know if he nickel and dimed his players with a flood of fines for being late, he may have been doing more damage than good.

His clever, diplomatic solution was to set the clock in a meeting room 15 minutes fast. One Packer star, Dave Robinson, recalled, "If he called a meeting for 1:00, he'd start that meeting at 12:45. If you came in at 12:50, you were five minutes 'late.' But you really were 10 minutes early from the time the meeting was [really] supposed to start. Therefore, he didn't have to fine you for being late."

One of the crazier stories of usurping a coach's power comes from the 1950s. Bert Rechichar was a versatile member of the Baltimore Colts who saw some strange things during his 10-year career. Dale Stewart said Rechichar shared one particular story about the game of football circa the 1950s. "He said they played games in which they would put themselves in. That is to say, if they didn't like the way the game was going, a player would just run on the field; and a coach is standing there on the sidelines, and he didn't even know what was going on." Presumably and hopefully, this took place during the exhibition season, but who knows how bizarre things could get back then.

Rechichar said, "Oh, hell, we'd go in and tell some rookie, 'Get outta' here. Go sit down.'" Stewart said that according to Rechichar, "There were games like that when we knew we could beat a damn team if we *didn't* listen to our coach. It was a wild time in the NFL way back then, weird, a wide open thing."

HOW DID HALL OF FAME QUARTERBACK BOBBY LAYNE DO SO WELL WHEN HE WAS SAID TO BE HUNGOVER OR DRUNK DURING SOME GAMES?

Bert Rechichar related a revealing story about Layne. "It was like he wouldn't play the game of football if he wasn't half lit, half high. He refused to wear a facemask. He'd say, 'I'm not wearing no damn facemask.' He'd get belted in the mouth, but he wouldn't feel it because he was half crocked. Then he'd throw a touchdown. He was high in every game, but he could throw a football."

Art "Fatso" Donovan, an all-time great Colt, had another tale of Layne. One game his line was letting him down. After one sack of Layne by Donovan, the defensive tackle noticed the stench of alcohol on Layne's breath. "You must have downed quite a few last night," Donovan said. Layne replied with a grin, "Fatso, let me let you in on a secret. The way this game was going, I had to down a few at halftime."

THERE HAVE BEEN MANY TRICK PLAYS, FROM THE STATUE OF LIBERTY TO THE PHILLY SPECIAL, BUT SOME HAVE BEEN ESPECIALLY CLEVER, DEVIOUS, AND NOTEWORTHY. START WITH AN OLDIE: HOW DID POP WARNER DECEIVE VIRTUALLY EVERYONE ON THE FIELD AND IN THE STANDS ONE DAY WITH A HIGHLY UNORTHODOX SCHEME?

Warner went so far as to tamper with his team's uniform's by having "elasticized bands sewn into his players' jerseys." After receiving a kickoff, his players quickly huddled together on the fly, obscuring their activity from the team covering the play. The player who had hauled in the kickoff quickly handed the football to a teammate. That player hid the ball under his jersey while he himself momentarily stayed hidden from everyone due to the cluster of teammates surrounding him. All of the players then scooted off in different directions. The baffled defense was caught in a sort of variation on the old "Button, button. Who's got the button" game.

Warner, in the same vein as Major League Baseball's trickiest person, Bill Veeck, could have argued that (as Veeck said many years later) he wasn't breaking any rules, he was "merely testing their elasticity."

HOW DID MIAMI DOLPHIN QUARTERBACK DAN MARINO CONCOCT A TRICK PLAY WHICH LED TO A SURPRISING AND UNFORGETTABLE TOUCHDOWN?

In November of 1994, Marino came up with a scheme to fool the New York Jets in what is called the "Fake Spike" game. With only 22 seconds left to play in the game, Miami trailed 24–21, but they were in control of the football at the Jets 8 yard line. Marino approached the line of scrimmage and gestured that he was about to spike the ball to stop the clock. He took the snap, *faked* a spike, then launched the ball to Mark Ingram for what proved to be the game-winning score. In a way, the Jets were caught napping, in that there was no real need for the Dolphins to kill the clock with a spike—they still had a timeout left which they could have used.

WHAT EMBARRASSING MISPLAY IS FORMER MINNESOTA VIKING JIM MARSHALL KNOWN FOR?

Fred Cox, who twice led the NFL in scoring, was a Minnesota teammate of Jim Marshall when the mammoth defensive end committed a huge, unforgettable blunder. Here's what Cox witnessed: With the Vikings up, 27–17, in the fourth quarter, Marshall recovered a San Francisco fumble and, confused, ran toward his own end zone, thinking he was about to score a touchdown.

Cox's reaction to seeing the play unfold was quite simple: "I was thinking, 'Jim, you're running the wrong way.' The greatest part of that whole situation was he was running the wrong way and he was so fast our defensive backs were chasing him but they couldn't catch him, and Fran Tarkenton is off the field running as hard as he can down the sidelines yelling at him, 'You're going the wrong way.' It was a comedy act.

"The only positive thing I can say is we ended up winning, 27–22. The two-point safety didn't enter into the game's outcome, but it provided a moment of levity never to be forgotten—and the play *could have* been a deciding one.

"The only reason it was two points and not six was he was so excited when he got into the end zone, he tossed the ball out of the end zone. If he had just dropped it on the ground the 49ers would have fallen on it for a touchdown. It was just a crazy event."

JIM MARSHALL SCOOPS UP A FUMBLE AGAINST THE 49ERS AND HEADS TOWARD THE END ZONE—THE WRONG END ZONE.
(Wikimedia Commons)

Marshall still holds the record for the most fumble recoveries ever with 30. Upon his retirement in 1979, he was also the record holder for the most consecutive starts by an NFL player, 270, and the most total games played with 282—no small feat for a man laboring in the rough and tumble trenches. He played in 20 complete seasons, a record for a defensive player. Darrell Green and Junior Seau also spent 20 seasons in the league, but not complete seasons.

Cox said, "Marshall was probably the greatest defensive football player in football annals who isn't in the Hall of Fame. He should be there. It's hard to believe that a man who played for all those years without missing a football game and was named to two All-Pro games isn't in the Hall of Fame. And it's strictly because we lost four Super Bowls."

WHO GOT THE AMERICAN FOOTBALL LEAGUE STARTED?

It was Lamar Hunt, who was the son of one of the richest men in the country, Texas oilman H. L. Hunt. In 1958, Lamar had a desire to bring pro football to Texas, but his efforts failed. Undaunted, a year later he thought, "Why not form a new football league?"

In August of 1959, Hunt and another Texas oilman named Bud Adams announced that two teams, Hunt's and the one owned by Adams, the Houston Oilers, had begun the process of the formation of the new league. The first season for the AFL was 1960 and Hunt's team, which later became the Kansas City Chiefs, settled in as the Dallas Texans.

Soon six other wealthy investors joined in what they called "The Foolish Club," putting up $25,000 per man to enjoy boasting rights that they owned a pro football club—even while realizing they might be tossing that sum of money away if the fledgling league should fold.

HOW WELL DID HUNT'S TEXANS DO AT FIRST?

Their first season's record, under future Hall of Fame coach Hank Stram, was 8-6, the third best record in the eight-team league. However, the new organization lost a reported $1 million in their first year of existence. A story has it that someone approached Lamar's father, pointing out what a large loss Lamar had just absorbed. H. L. Hunt replied something along the lines of, "Well, at that rate, he'll go broke in another 100 years."

Still, the NFL is said to have retaliated against Hunt and the AFL by giving an expansion franchise to Dallas in 1960, hoping the new Cowboys' presence in the Lone Star State would hurt, and perhaps cause the destruction of, the Texans.

Ultimately, the AFL forced the NFL to merge, and Hunt, for those concerned, certainly did not go bankrupt. Longtime AFL coach John Madden said, "I got my first coaching opportunity in the American Football League, and I know if it weren't for Lamar Hunt there wouldn't have been an American Football League. Every time I ever saw him, I thanked him."

WHAT WAS THE PREVALENT THINKING AMONG COACHES REGARDING CONCUSSIONS BEFORE DOCTORS BEGAN TO ENLIGHTEN EVERYONE ABOUT HOW DANGEROUS FOOTBALL WAS CONCERNING HEAD INJURIES? AND HOW HAS INTENTIONAL HELMET-TO-HELMET CONTACT CHANGED OVER THE YEARS?

Dale Stewart played fullback for the Carnegie Tech (now Carnegie Mellon) Tartans mainly in the late 1950s. He vividly recalls the way head injuries were dealt with back then. "We never had a concussion," he said. "Someone would hold up four fingers and ask us how many fingers we saw. You'd say three, and they'd say, 'Close enough.'" And it was back into the game the dazed player would go. "I never even heard the word *concussion*, but I know I had some. I saw stars. You'd walk around and not even know where you were going—sometimes to the wrong huddle.

"They taught you to lead with your helmet. 'Put your helmet into his numbers.' What if their coach was saying the same thing? Then it's helmet to helmet. How much head-to-head explosions do you think we had?"

In Raymond Berry's autobiography, *All the Moves I Had*, he wrote, "We played a physical game, but back then concussions weren't a big topic." He first became aware of how serious they were in 1953 when his Southern Methodist University played a team which had "a player or two that started using the head gear into the face. From that point on I started seeing it again, but just periodically."

Berry said he could not remember ever seeing an NFL player purposely slam their head gear into an opponent's face. "It was not a part of the NFL culture then even though we had some of the greatest, toughest defensive players of all time."

Even during his NFL coaching years that stretched through 1992, the brutal tactic was very rare. "However, one particular team introduced the deliberate, illegal use of head gear around the 1970s, I think. That's when all this business about concussions started happening. It started escalating and it spread down to college football. Coaches began teaching it, and it became a part of the game with a great many players."

Berry decried the type of coach who said, "'Put your hat on him! Put your hat on him!' Meaning hit him with the helmet. It's an epidemic. And all these coaches who say that never had a hat put in *their* face. It's unnecessary and extremely damaging, dangerous, and it has long-lasting effects on multiple players.

"The helmet is an unforgiving blunt instrument. You might as well take a sledge hammer to somebody as a helmet." He felt the NFL did nothing about such dirty tactics for too long. Fortunately, that look-the-other way attitude has vanished and new, strict rules have come into being to protect players.

WHO WAS RECOGNIZED AS THE WORLD'S FASTEST HUMAN WHILE ALSO PLAYING IN THE NFL FROM 1965 THROUGH 1975 AS A WIDE RECEIVER AND PUNT AND KICKOFF-RETURN ARTIST, PRIMARILY WITH THE DALLAS COWBOYS?

The speed burner is Hall of Famer Bob Hayes, the man who is said to have changed the way defenses play. Because no defensive back could conceivably keep up with Hayes, the zone defense came into being.

Nicknamed Bullet Bob, he reportedly turned in a time of 5.28 seconds in a 60-yard run, and a 9.1 time for a 100-yard stretch. He never lost a 100-yard or a 100-meter dash throughout his entire college days at Florida A & M or as an Olympian. He won a gold medal in Tokyo for the 100-meter dash and tied the world's record while wearing borrowed spikes. His 8.8-second time is still the fastest ever for a 100-meter relay runner. He is also the only man ever to win an Olympic gold medal (two, actually) and a Super Bowl ring.

BOB HAYES LED THE NFL IN RECEIVING TOUCHDOWNS HIS FIRST TWO SEASONS IN THE LEAGUE. (Wikimedia Commons)

In retrospect, it's hard to fathom how low he was drafted. The Dallas Cowboys didn't choose him until the seventh round, and the AFL Broncos waited until the 14th round to make him the 105th overall pick in the 1964 draft.

WHICH NFL PLAYERS OF THIS CHAPTER'S TIMEFRAME WERE KNOWN FOR THEIR ACCOMPLISHMENTS IN OTHER, MUCH LESS PHYSICAL ENDEAVORS?

Three NFL players were also Rhodes Scholars. Pat Haden became an attorney and a partner in an equity firm. Byron "Whizzer" White became an associate justice of the Supreme Court from 1962 to 1993. The third man on the list, though not from this chapter's era, is Myron Rolle, who went on to become a doctor. As an aside, Rolle had five cousins who played in the NFL—Chad and Keyshawn Johnson, and Antrel, Samari, and Brian Rolle.

Frank Ryan was not only a gifted quarterback (1958–1970), he was also another type of doctor. Ryan, who primarily played for the Cleveland Browns, earned his doctorate from Rice. He was a member of the Case Western Reserve University faculty from 1967 to 1974 after teaching at Rice during his playing days. At one point, he taught math in morning sessions then hustled on to afternoon football practice sessions.

Sportswriter Red Smith joked that the Cleveland Browns offense under Ryan was made up of the quarterback "who understood Einstein's theory of relativity and ten teammates who didn't know there was one." How smart was Ryan? He came up

AFTER FOOTBALL, JACK KEMP HAD A LONG CAREER IN POLITICS. (Department of Housing and Urban Development via Wikimedia Commons)

with a dissertation which had a title most people can't even begin to decipher—"Characterization of the Set of Asymptotic Values of a Function Holomorphic in the Unit Disc."

One player who turned to dentistry was Les Horvath, the 1944 Heisman Trophy winner who spent three years as an NFL running back. Another man who practiced dentistry, including having some Baltimore Colts as patients, was Sam Havrilak, who spent 1969 through 1973 with the Colts. By the way, Hall of Fame tight end Mike Ditka studied dentistry at the University of Pittsburgh, which led to the great line that said he wound up dishing out "thundering blocks and stiff arms . . . knocking out the very teeth he had hoped to one day examine."

All-Pro defensive tackle Mike Reid played five NFL seasons, all with the Cincinnati Bengals. He also played the piano with tremendous talent, appearing with some symphony orchestras at times. Reid even wrote a Ronnie Milsap song, "Stranger in My House," which won the 1984 Grammy Award for Best Country Song. He wrote for other stars such as Tim McGraw, Willie Nelson, and Wynonna Judd. Reid even hit the charts as a solo singer with seven songs, and one of them, "Walk on Faith," reached the top spot on the country charts in February of 1991.

Alan Page made it to four Super Bowls as a member of the Vikings. He also made it big, becoming an associate justice of the Minnesota Supreme Court from 1993 until 2015.

The world of politics welcomed quarterback Jack Kemp as a US congressman for nine terms from 1971 to 1989. Kemp, who gained football fame as a star from 1957 through 1969 mainly for the Buffalo Bills, also went on to become the running mate for presidential candidate Bob Dole in 1996.

WHY WAS THE 1983 NFL DRAFT SO REMARKABLE?

That draft produced the "quarterback class of 1983," when six QBs (ranging in talent from solid to great) were taken in the first round. Todd Blackledge went to the Chiefs and Ken O'Brien was the Jets pick. The other four, who all went on to play in at least one Super Bowl, were Jim Kelly (Buffalo's choice in 1983, but he spent time in the United States Football League before finally joining the Bills); John Elway (drafted by Baltimore, but with Denver for his entire 16-year career); Dan Marino (Miami); and Tony Eason (New England).

Oddly, over the first 14 seasons of the men mentioned above who played in at least one Super Bowl game, their composite record there was 0-9. Only Elway's two Super Bowl wins later salvaged the combined record a bit. Plus, three of the worst shellackings suffered in Super Bowl play featured Elway (a 55–10 loss), Eason (a 46–10 defeat), and Kelly (52–17).

Coincidentally, all six were drafted by teams out of the American Football Conference. Not at all coincidentally, half of them went on to become Hall of Famers—Elway, Marino, and Kelly.

WHO WERE SOME OF THE BEST RUNNING BACKS IN THIS CHAPTER'S ERA AT EXECUTING THE HALFBACK OPTION, A PLAY IN WHICH A RUNNING BACK CAN EITHER RUN OR PASS THE BALL DOWNFIELD?

Paul Hornung came to the Green Bay Packers via the University of Notre Dame, where he was a Heisman Award–winning quarterback, so it's not surprising that he often threw the halfback option pass in the NFL. He once threw two TD passes (of his career five touchdown passes) in a game versus the Los Angeles Rams, something only accomplished two other times—by men with no quarterbacking experience, Gene Mingo and Walter Payton. One year, Coach Vince Lombardi had Hornung throw the ball 16 times in 12 games.

Dan Reeves also was a college quarterback. At South Carolina he was a three-year starter who threw for 2,561 yards, so he also knew how to handle a football. As a Dallas Cowboy running back, one year he averaged a sky high 26.4 yards gained on every one of his completions.

All-American Tom Matte was the Ohio State quarterback for the 1959 and 1960 seasons, but that school under Coach Woody Hayes wasn't known for passing much. Matte averaged just eight passes per game as a Buckeye. The famous line of Hayes, "Three yards and a cloud of dust," wasn't his motto for nothing, as he loved to pound the ball on the ground over and over again, churning out yards which led to many inexorable scoring drives which in turn led to almost inevitable wins.

Still, Matte had passing skills and when an emergency arose with his Colts in 1965, when the number one and two quarterbacks, Johnny Unitas and Gary Cuozzo, went down with injuries, Matte admirably took over quarterback chores. He won his only regular-season start to end the 1965 season, then, thrust into postseason play, he went 5-for-12 in an overtime loss to Green Bay. If the referee's call on the Don Chandler kick discussed earlier had been made correctly, Matte and the Colts, and not the Packers, would have advanced to the title game. What a storyline that would have been: an emergency quarterback playing for the NFL championship!

Like Matte, Dick Hoak played two positions in college, quarterback and running back, doing so at Penn State. In the NFL he was limited to action as a runner. That is, until the option pass was called for. Then his passing prowess came into play again. With the Steelers from 1961 through 1970, his completion rate was a laudable 50 percent.

Some say the first time the halfback option was employed was in 1910 by a College of Emporia player under the instruction of his coach, Homer Woodson Hargiss. Better chronicled are much more recent option passes such as the first running back to throw a touchdown pass in a Super Bowl. That distinction belongs to Dallas fullback Robert Newhouse in Super Bowl XII. His scoring strike was a key play in the Cowboys' victory over Denver.

Hall of Famer Walter Payton holds the NFL record for touchdown passes by a running back, with eight. More recently, LaDainian Tomlinson showed off his accurate arm by throwing seven touchdown passes in only 12 career halfback option plays.

HOW MANY QUARTERBACKS HAVE CAUGHT A TOUCHDOWN PASS IN A SUPER BOWL CONTEST?

In Super Bowl XXII, the Broncos' John Elway became the first quarterback in the history of the Super Bowl to catch a touchdown pass when he corralled a pass from halfback Steve Sewell.

Many years later, in Super Bowl LII, the Philadelphia Eagles were in a fourth and goal situation with 38 seconds left in the first half. They went for it employing a clever trick play. Quarterback Nick Foles lined up in the shotgun formation then shifted to a slot just before the ball was snapped to running back Corey Clement. He then flipped the ball to receiver Trey Burton to start an apparent end around. Instead, he lobbed the ball to a wide open Foles in the end zone.

Foles, who threw for three touchdowns and 373 yards to guide the Eagles to a 41–33 win over Tom Brady and the Patriots, was named the game's MVP.

WHICH COACHES HAVE MANAGED TO TAKE TWO DIFFERENT TEAMS TO A SUPER BOWL?

Most of the six men to achieve this did so mainly in the 20th century. Dick Vermeil took his Philadelphia Eagles to a Super Bowl and 19 years later returned to the big game once more with the St. Louis Rams. Dan Reeves led both the Denver Broncos and Atlanta Falcons to a total of four Super Bowls. Don Shula lost Super Bowl III to Joe Namath's New York Jets, but he also took the Miami Dolphins to five Super Bowls. Bill Parcells was in three Super Bowls with his Giants and Patriots. John Fox guided Carolina to the title game and 10 years later he took Denver to the Super Bowl. Finally, Mike Holmgren's Packers won it all in 1996 then lost the following season's Super Bowl. He made it back to coach the NFC champion Seahawks into a Super Bowl as well.

WHY DID DON SHULA, ONE OF THE GREATEST COACHES EVER, LEAVE THE FIRST TEAM HE SERVED AS A HEAD COACH, THE BALTIMORE COLTS?

Looking over his career stats, it's hard to imagine him being with more than one team, but that's life in the world of pro sports. Ideally, purists believe a legend such as Shula or, say, a Willie Mays should be with only one team for their entire career.

Shula's statistics and achievements include winning the most games ever as a head coach—his record stands at 347-173-6; only he and George Halas ever topped the 300-win plateau. Over Shula's seven seasons with the Colts, he never experienced a losing season. He posted a 12-2 season, a 10-3-1 season, and in the two years before his final one with the Colts, he went 11-1-2, and 13-1 to earn a trip to Super Bowl III. Overall, he experienced just two losing seasons during his 33-year NFL career. His teams made the playoffs 20 times and they won 10 or more games on 21 occasions.

So, again, why did he leave the Colts in the first place? The *Baltimore Sun* reported that a rift developed between team owner Carroll Rosenbloom and Shula because of the Colts' loss to the Jets in Super Bowl III. The season following that loss, Shula's record dropped off to 8-5-1.

In a 2008 interview, Shula said Rosenbloom's friends from New York "never let him forget [the heavily favored Colts' loss], and he never let me forget it." Shula felt that if he had defeated the Jets and continued his winning ways with the Colts, "I'd still be in Baltimore, eating crab cakes."

Cast off by Rosenbloom, Shula moved on to coach Miami where he went 10-4 in 1970, then took the Dolphins to three consecutive Super Bowls with a combined regular-season record of 36-5-1. His Dolphins won it all for the 1972 and 1973 seasons with a perfect record of 17-0 in 1972. That gave Shula a grand total of 44 wins and only six losses from 1971 through 1973. In fact, over his first six seasons with the Dolphins he averaged winning 11 games per year. During that same time period, the Colts did win one Super Bowl, but had a cumulative record which was just over the break-even point at 42-41-1. That had to give Rosenbloom some second thoughts for years, even when he moved on to become the principal owner of the Rams in 1972.

WHAT HALL OF FAME DEFENSIVE TACKLE—WHO PLAYED FROM 1958 THROUGH 1970 EXCLUSIVELY FOR THE DETROIT LIONS—HAD SUCH POOR VISION, IT WAS A MIRACLE HE COULD MAKE TACKLES ON BALL-CARRIERS HE COULD SEE ONLY AS BLURS AS HE CLOSED IN ON THEM?

Off the field Alex Karras had to wear thick glasses and he "was known to tackle anything or anyone at any time. If it wasn't the player carrying the football, he'd blame it on his eyes." Make no mistake, though, he was good. In fact, as an Iowa Hawkeye in 1957, he finished second in the Heisman voting, which put him in a tie for the highest ranking by any college lineman ever.

Karras was a three-time All-Pro who had four relatives who also made it to the NFL: brothers Lou and Ted, as well as Ted's son and grandson. Alex's grandnephew Ted was with the New England Patriots in 2021 as an offensive guard. At least one member of the family has been in the NFL in five decades.

Alex left football after the 1970 season and began an acting career. He first gained attention by playing himself while still an active player in the 1968 movie *Paper Lion*. Six years later, he *really*

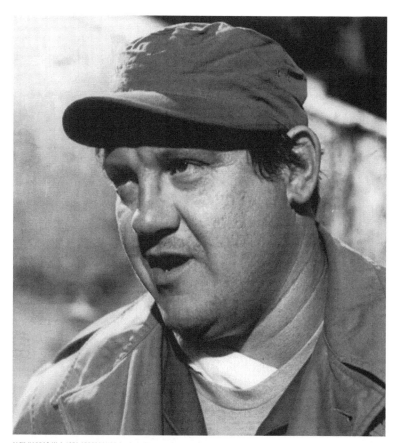

ALEX KARRAS IN A 1974 APPEARANCE ON THE HIT TELEVISION SHOW *M*A*S*H* (Wikimedia Commons)

gained notice when he played the not very bright, outlaw character Mongo in the comedy *Blazing Saddles*. His television series *Webster* was such a hit, it ran for 150 episodes. He even entertained viewers as a *Monday Night Football* analyst. For example, there was the time he was covering a game played on a cold night and the image of the intimidating Raiders defensive end Otis Sistrunk appeared on the screen with steam emitting from his bald head. Seeing this, Karras pointed out how "far out" Sistrunk was by saying he was "from the University of Mars."

Karras was inducted into the Pro Football Hall of Fame in 2020.

WHY DID KARRAS, AS WELL AS ANOTHER HALL OF FAMER, PAUL HORNUNG OF THE GREEN BAY PACKERS, HAVE TO SIT OUT THE ENTIRE 1963 SEASON?

While the NFL now has a team based in Las Vegas, and the league even sanctions sportsbooks, gambling was a taboo to the extreme long ago—so much so that two of the game's biggest names, Karras and Hornung, along with a few lesser known players who were fined, were punished. The two stars were suspended indefinitely with a chance to be reinstated after one year, which is what took place.

Hornung did bet on NFL games, at times as much as what was then a hefty $500. He even bet on his own team, the Packers, but only placed wagers for them to win. Karras, who had partial ownership of a Detroit bar frequented by gamblers, was also punished for "associating with undesirables," and "known hoodlums." Karras placed at least six bets of $50 or $100 on NFL games, once wagering on a Lions game. During his suspension, Karras made $17,000, a figure that exceeded his salary with the Lions, by taking part in a pro wrestling match.

Sports Illustrated writer Jon Wertheim observed of commissioner Pete Rozelle's verdict, "This would be the equivalent of, say Aaron Rodgers and J.J. Watt both getting pounded with a

16-game suspension for a 'sin.'" And that "sin," he noted, was one "that would later become as much a part of the NFL tableau as tailgating and the Super Bowl halftime show."

In 2019, when Hornung was on hand to cut the ribbon on a new Indiana sportsbook and to place "a ceremonial first bet," it was rather ironic, but otherwise no big deal. It's also ironic that as part of the reinstatements for Karras and Hornung, both men had to agree they would not visit Las Vegas. Upon returning to the NFL, a bitter Karras went to midfield for a coin toss prior to a game. When the official asked him to make the heads or tails call, Karras refused saying, "I'm sorry, sir, but I'm not permitted to gamble."

WHAT STANDOUT KICKER FROM THIS CHAPTER'S ERA INVENTED THE NERF FOOTBALL?

Fred Cox led a multifaceted life. After his playing days with the Minnesota Vikings were over, he became an aviator. He also went on to become a chiropractor, earning roughly $100,000 a year, which he said was about twice as much money as he was paid in the NFL.

Cox also invented a safe, soft football which became the Parker Brothers toy, the Nerf football, which made its debut in 1972. That venture earned him rich royalties for years. In a 1997 interview, Cox said that more than 50 million of the footballs had been sold, with a one-year high of six or seven million. He pointed out the average life span of toys is five years, but his invention keeps on going.

Cox, who played his entire 15-year career with the Vikings, led the league in scoring twice, and he was among the top ten in that category 10 times. Even though he retired in 1977, he still ranks 36th for career points and field goals made. He remains the leading scorer in Vikings history, too, with 1,365 points, more than twice as many points as the number two man on the list, Cris Carter.

As skilled as he was, unbelievably, as a high school kicker he was never put in a game to attempt a field goal, and as a college player at Pitt he had only four field goal attempts—and *none* until his senior season at Pitt when he kicked three of his four field goals in one game against Notre Dame. By way of contrast, as a pro, he attempted more field goals than all but 21 NFL players ever.

Interestingly, Cox grew up on the same street in his hometown of Monongahela, Pennsylvania, as a young boy who visited Cox's parents' grocery store on occasion. That boy grew up to become one of the greatest quarterbacks in the league's history, Joe Montana.

WHAT PART OF THE UNITED STATES HAS PRODUCED SO MANY HALL OF FAME QUARTERBACKS THAT IT EARNED THE NICKNAME "AMERICA'S CRADLE OF QUARTERBACKS"?

Almost one out of every four quarterbacks of the modern era who are enshrined in Canton, Ohio, hail from an area of western Pennsylvania that lies within a radius of about 60 miles around Pittsburgh—six of the 27 quarterbacks, to be precise.

Not long ago, the entire population of Pennsylvania represented only about 4 percent of the country's total population. For a small sliver of that state to be responsible for such a disproportionate percentage of Hall of Fame quarterbacks is simply incredible.

The six legends are George Blanda, Johnny Unitas, Joe Namath, Joe Montana, Dan Marino, and Jim Kelly. According to the book *America's Football Factory*, from 1949 until the start of the next century, at least one of the six greats was active in the NFL with the exception of 1978 (between Joe Namath's retirement and the rookie season of the next baton carrier, Joe Montana). That's a period of 50 out of 51 years with one or more of the greatest western Pennsylvania quarterbacks being an NFL fixture.

At least one of the six greats took part in 13 of the first 48 Super Bowls, and they even accounted for AFL and NFL titles earlier in the 50s and into the 60s.

The best Pennsylvania high school players are selected to play in the Big 33 Football Classic, a sort of all-star game which dates back to 1957. At least one player from each of the first 43 Super Bowls also played in that contest, including Namath, Montana, and Marino.

Upon their retirement, all six of the quarterbacks were in the top 12 for career touchdown passes, and five of them were in the top 10. Four of them also ranked in the top 10 for their percentage of completions. Furthermore, both Unitas and Marino finished their careers as the top passer of all time for total completions, yards, and touchdown passes.

WHO IS CONSIDERED TO BE THE BEST SCRAMBLING QUARTERBACK OF THE 1922 THROUGH 1999 ERA?

Many observers would go with Fran Tarkenton. Viking teammate Fred Cox said that there was no question in his mind that Tarkenton was more proficient at scrambling than Roger Staubauch. "That's not taking anything away from Staubach—he was a great quarterback, but he wasn't even in Francis's league as far as being able to scramble."

There's no doubt Tarkenton frustrated many a burly lineman who vainly tried to latch onto the elusive quarterback only to wind up huffing and puffing and, no doubt, cussing out Sir Francis.

In the book *Remembering the Stars of the NFL Glory Years*, Tarkenton is credited as having "revolutionized the quarterback position when he defied the prevailing convention that quarterbacks had to stay in the pocket in order to succeed. He divested himself of tacklers with the same ease as he shooed flies away."

Another western Pennsylvania native, Myron Pottios, was one of many linebackers who dreaded facing Tarkenton. "Here's Tarkenton—you've got him all boxed in. Next thing, he's scrambling all over and he breaks loose and hits a guy downfield for 40 yards and keeps a drive going. Those are the things that drive you nuts because there's nothing that you can do—you had the perfect defense called and everybody plays it perfectly, but because of his scrambling ability, he was able to disrupt it and make your perfect defense a no defense.

"He affected you mentally because you better get ready because you know you're going to be running all over the place, especially our defensive linemen. They said, 'Holy hell.' Psychologically, they knew what was going to happen. Once he started scrambling, they got to chase him all over, and that's when you get hit. When you're trying to chase him, you get a blind shot and those hurt."

Miami Dolphin offensive lineman Doug Crusan, yet another product of western Pennsylvania, was in awe of Tarkenton's talent, too. "When our defensive linemen were done playing the Vikings, they were thoroughly exhausted. He ran *all over the place*. You'd chase him and chase him. They'd go, 'You gotta' be kidding,' because he would get back in the pocket, and then he's gone. He scrambled all the time, more than Staubach—he was always in motion."

Most experts go with Tarkenton as the best, but give a tip of the hat to Staubach, whose very nickname of Roger the Dodger attests to his uncanny ability to scramble.

WHO IS THE ONLY MAN EVER TO AVERAGE MORE THAN 100 YARDS PER GAME OVER AN ENTIRE CAREER?

Barry Sanders of the Detroit Lions came tantalizingly close to that mark at 99.8. He rolled on and on for 15,269 yards over a marvelous career (1989 through 1998). One season, 1997, his yards gained per game total was tops in the NFL for the fourth time—this time at a fantastic 128.3 yards. He led the NFL in rushing in his second season, and he was still a whiz in his final five seasons, accumulating 8,480 yards with 2,053 of those yards coming in his next-to-last season. He never ran for fewer than 1,115 yards, and he averaged 1,527 yards per season.

Despite Sanders's heroics, the answer to this question is Jim Brown. He managed to bang out 104.3 yards every single game for 118 games over his nine-year career, racking up a grand total of 12,312 yards. He retired early, at the age of 29 and still in his prime. The proof of that is in his final season he galloped for 1,544, the second highest total of his career. The most he ran for in a year? That would be his 1,863 he collected in his next-to-next-to last season.

The litany of his accomplishments go on and on, but consider a few more. He led the NFL in rushing in every season he played, save 1962 when he still rushed for 996 yards. He also led the league in yards gained per game every season but one, once

JIM BROWN'S 1959 TOPPS CARD (Wikimedia Commons)

averaging 133.1 yards for every contest he played, which remains the second best average ever. In his final season he led the NFL in touchdowns for the fifth time, hitting paydirt 17 times in 14 games.

Brown's lifetime totals would have been higher if he hadn't played the first four seasons of his career when teams were still only playing 12 games each year. People still shake their heads in disbelief when they wonder what his stats would be if he played today's schedule.

SPEAKING OF SANDERS, JUST HOW DEDICATED TO HIS GAME WAS HE?

Bill Keenist, who was in the Detroit Lions front office in various capacities for many years observed, "I saw every one of his runs and nobody could do what he did with the football. He could go two different directions at the same time."

As for Sanders and his motivation to excel, Keenist shared what he called, "My all-time favorite story about Barry. It resonates with anyone in any walk of life about work ethic and the football ethic he always displayed. And they say character is truly revealed when no one's watching."

The tale begins when Sanders was preparing for the final game of the 1996 season. The Lions, who had lost eight of their last nine games, had nothing to play for. Phoning in a weak performance could have been somewhat understandable, but that was not Sanders's style.

Keenist was told to get a quote from Sanders for the media, so he sought him out after a practice session. Many of the other Lions had already gone home, but Keenist found Sanders in the weight room. "Here's the greatest player in the NFL, and he's in there getting one last workout in."

Sanders asked Keenist to wait for him to finish his workout. Some time later Keenist returned, only to find the weight room empty. It turns out Sanders, not quite satisfied to call his workout over, had returned to the football field. "I took a look out at the dimly lit field, and there was a single, solitary figure running sprints at midfield. It gives me chills to this day when I think of that."

Sanders's dedication paid off. During the game which soon followed, Detroit had to battle the 11-4 San Francisco 49ers, who boasted the number one NFC defense against the rush. "Barry was around 160 yards behind Terrell Davis for the NFL rushing title. No one expected Barry to even come close—no one but Barry, his teammates, and anyone who knew him. He put 175 yards on the 49er defense to win the rushing title."

WHO WAS THE PLACEKICKER WHO STUNNED THE NFL WHEN HE KICKED A THEN-RECORD 63-YARD FIELD GOAL TO WIN A GAME AT THE END OF REGULATION?

Tom Dempsey is the kicker who made history back on November 8, 1970. He was a man whose story was even more astonishing because he was born with no toes on his kicking foot and no fingers on his right hand. He was permitted to wear a special, modified kicking shoe which had "a flattened and enlarged toe surface." Some people wondered if that gave him an advantage—was his record tainted? When asked by reporters if using the shoe was unfair, Dempsey replied, "Unfair, eh? How 'bout you try kickin' a 63 yard field goal to win it with two seconds left an' yer wearin' a square shoe, oh yea, and no toes either."

Years later, an analysis of the shoe concluded Dempsey did not have an advantage—if anything, the smaller area where he could make contact with the football may have been a disadvantage.

Dempsey's Saints were trailing, 17–16, to the Lions when they lined up for the long-distance kick with time on the scoreboard about to expire. Lions star defensive tackle Alex Karras reportedly scoffed at the sight of the Saints formation, and felt there was no need to even put a serious rush on the kicker because, surely even

New Orleans wasn't serious about the field goal attempt. After all, who tries a kick when the line of scrimmage is a team's own 37 yard line?

Dempsey not only set a new record, he smashed the old mark by 7 yards. The old record belonged to the Baltimore Colts' Bert Rechichar, who was primarily a defensive back/placekicker. His booming 56-yard kick had carried over the end zone's back line to break a 17-year-old record—and he did it wearing a regular soft-toed football shoe, not a kicking shoe. Not only that, as unbelievable as it sounds, the record-setting kick was his *first* NFL attempt ever.

Of course, the current record for the longest field goal belongs to Justin Tucker, a 66-yard, last-second, game-winning blast. That shattered Matt Prater's 64-yard field goal for the Broncos in 2013.

It's a little known fact, but the record, as of 2020, for the longest field goal kicked by a high school player is a jaw-dropping 68 yards. In 1985, Dirk Borgognone, who had been trained to kick using the old straight-on method, crushed the record-setting kick while playing for Reno High School in Nevada. At that time it was the longest field goal kicked by *anyone* in NCAA and NFL play. An NAIA kicker named Ove Johansson was the only player with a longer field goal, 69 yards, than Borgognone. For some reason, Borgognone's coach used him only on kicks of 50+ yards after his record-setting field goal. The result was, after missing his next eight long attempts, his 68-yarder was the last field goal he made at Reno High.

When he moved on to the University of the Pacific, he was hampered by a rule change. Accustomed to kicking (legally) off a tee, an NCAA rule banning that device affected his ability. Still, in 1995, Borgognone wound up playing in the NFL when Green Bay needed a kicker to fill in for their normal starter. He lasted two games, but he only got onto the field for eight kickoffs.

HOW ARE THE RULES ON PASS INTERFERENCE DIFFERENT IN COLLEGE BALL FROM THE NFL?

At the NFL level, aside from pass interference in the end zone, if a defensive back is guilty of this penalty, the team on offense is given an automatic first down at the spot of the infraction.

Imagine that the Pittsburgh Steelers have the ball on their own 1 yard line. Their quarterback heaves a long pass down to the 1 yard line of the New England Patriots. Yes, one has to have a very lively imagination to conjure up a picture of a pass traveling that far, but for the sake of exaggerating a point, go with it. A New England defender is called for pass interference, and that will cost the Patriots 98 yards and, in all probability, a score.

Now, in the college game if the same situation as above played out, the maximum penalty would normally be a measly advance of the football 15 yards. That means that in most cases, a college defensive back seeing that he was about to be burned for a sure touchdown, could virtually mug a receiver knowing the slap on the wrist penalty which would ensue is nothing compared to giving up six points.

Such a mugging is exactly what took place in the College Football Playoff National Championship when the Georgia Bulldogs defeated the Alabama Crimson Tide on January 10, 2022. In the fourth quarter of that contest Alabama had an 18–13 lead when Georgia quarterback Stetson Bennett fired a deep pass intended for Jermaine Burton, who had defender Khyree Jackson badly beaten. A reception and a jaunt into the end zone seemed inevitable when Johnson literally tackled Burton, gladly willing to give up 15 yards to save six points.

Mike Liner, who spent 35 years as a line judge in the college ranks, gave his take on the college rule in the book *You're the Ref.* "That very [NFL example] play you described, that's a game-changer. I mean, [under NFL rules] you just gave them 98 yards on your penalty. The official has got to say, 'Look, was that really bad enough to give them 98 yards?' But now [in college ball] you can say, 'That was pass interference; we're going to give them 15 and a first down.'

"You put the thing in perspective. Let's make the penalty commensurate with the foul. That's the deal. You want the thing called, and the way you make it called is you don't absolutely take the other team's head off. That call is like the death penalty. If you're on the jury and you're giving somebody 20 years or death, it's easier to give them 20 years. You're going to make that call, but it's hard to make the death penalty call."

WHEN AND HOW DID THE AFL GAIN CREDIBILITY, AND THEIR FIRST TASTE OF EQUALITY WITH THE NFL?

Many experts feel that a major turning point in the direction the AFL took occurred when that league managed to lure colorful Joe Namath away from the NFL. Both the St. Louis Cardinals and the Jets drafted Namath in the first round of the leagues' 1965 drafts. Jets owner Sonny Werblin dangled a three-year $427,000 contract in front of him, which represented a new record for a pro football deal. Namath signed and gave added credibility to the AFL. One year later, the two leagues announced they would merge in 1970.

The palpable feeling that the AFL truly *belonged* and could hang with the NFL came when the younger of the two leagues began to win Super Bowls. That began as early as just the third Super Bowl when Namath and the Jets upset, some say totally astounded, the powerful Baltimore Colts.

By the fourth Super Bowl, a win by Kansas City from the AFL over Minnesota gave the AFL as many Super Bowl wins as NFL teams. The next year was the first season of play after the official merger, and the one, now combined league in existence, called the NFL, split into teams from the American Football Conference (AFC) and the National Football Conference (NFC).

JOE NAMATH DURING HIS ROOKIE SEASON WITH THE JETS (Wikimedia Commons)

Three teams from the "old" NFL moved into the AFC: the Colts, the Cleveland Browns, and the Pittsburgh Steelers. Before long, the idea of teams from the AFL being inferior was cast aside.

HOW MANY PLAYOFF GAMES DID JOE NAMATH WIN AFTER THE SUPER BOWL UPSET?

After winning Super Bowl III, Namath never won another play-off game. After winning the AFL East Division in 1968, his Jets had to play only one game, the AFL championship game (a tight 27–23 win over Oakland), to reach the Super Bowl. That's quite unlike the many tiers of games teams must survive to make it to the title game today.

After Namath's Super Bowl win, and with two games and a 2-0 postseason record behind him, the following season he again reached the playoffs. This time the Jets, led by their 26-year-old quarterback, fell by a 13–6 score to Kansas City. So, Namath saw playoff action in two of his first five seasons, and he owned an overall 21-7 regular-season record over his two playoff years. From then through 1977, though, his teams never again had a record better than 7-6 with him starting.

WHY DO SOME PEOPLE BELIEVE THAT NAMATH'S STATISTICS ARE NOT WORTHY OF HALL OF FAME STATUS?

Fred Cox called Namath "a riverboat gambler type of quarter-back—he would throw into double coverage more than any guy I ever saw. Fran Tarkenton and I talked about this a lot, but Namath got away with it a lot. And it wasn't that he was a bad quarterback; he was a good quarterback, but if you're going to categorize him, he'd be number five on my list." Cox was referring to the list of six Hall of Fame quarterbacks from the Pittsburgh vicinity mentioned earlier: George Blanda, number six on Cox's list, Johnny Unitas, Dan Marino, Joe Montana, Jim Kelly, and Namath. Cox concluded that it bothered him that "Namath had more interceptions [220] than he had touchdown passes [173]."

Namath, in fact, led his league in passes picked off four times with totals of 28, 28, 27, and 22—and those stats all took place during 14-game seasons. It may also come as a jolt to some, but his career win-loss record as a starting quarterback reveals he lost more games than he won (62-63-1).

As will be covered later, Namath's lifetime quarterback rating is the third worst among all Hall of Fame QBs. Still, he is always remembered for the win in Super Bowl III, and he certainly did impress enough people to earn Hall of Fame status. After all, he also accomplished things like becoming the first quarterback to throw for more than 4,000 yards—and he was the only passer to do this during a 14-game schedule.

Finally, as former LA Rams defensive end Fred Dryer said in an HBO documentary on Namath, "That guy was very important to the game of football as a cultural icon, and how he brought professional football into the television era and with it a whole degree of excitement. . . . The likes of him will never ever, ever pass this way again."

WHICH RUNNING BACK REPLACED JIM BROWN, AND HOW DID HE COMPARE TO THE CLEVELAND LEGEND?

Even though Leroy Kelly went on to carve out a Hall of Fame career, it can be argued that nobody can truly replace or be compared to Brown. Still, Kelly did a pretty good imitation of Brown.

During Kelly's first two seasons he carried the ball just 43 times. The next year, 1966, with Brown departed, Kelly led the NFL with his 5.5 yards per rush average, with his 1,141 yards, and his 15 touchdowns. The next two seasons he exploded for 1,205 and 1,239 yards to top the league. Furthermore, he led the NFL for ground touchdowns three consecutive seasons (1966–1968). He wound up with 7,274 yards rushing and 90 total TDs over eight full seasons. For the record, Brown compiled 12,312 yards and 126 touchdowns over nine seasons.

Kelly's brother Pat, a highly religious man, played Major League Baseball for 15 years. He provided what turned out to be a great straight line for his Baltimore Orioles manager Earl Weaver. Trying to spread the ways and the word of the Bible to Weaver, Kelly said, "Earl, it's great to walk with the Lord, it's great to walk with Jesus." Weaver replied, "I'd rather have you walk with the bases loaded."

WHAT WAS THE NAME OF THE POSTSEASON GAME THAT WAS HELD TO DETERMINE THE THIRD- AND FOURTH-PLACE TEAMS IN THE NFL, AND DURING WHAT YEARS DID THE GAME TAKE PLACE?

From 1960 through 1969, the NFL actually thought it was a good idea to hold an exhibition game to determine the third and fourth place teams for each season. At first the game was held between the two teams which wound up in second place in each of the two conferences. In 1967, when the NFL divided the conferences into four divisions—the Capitol, Century, Coastal, and Central divisions—the two teams which lost the East and the West conference title games met in the Playoff Bowl.

The vying for the right to be called the third best team of the season was the same basic scheme NCAA basketball had used, hosting a consolation game from 1946 until 1981. However, it's difficult to imagine too many of the NFL players getting excited about being a part of the Playoff Bowl. For that matter, many didn't even want to take part in the game. After all, if you couldn't attain the goal of winning the championship or at least making it to that top game, who cares if you can shout a hollow boast of, "We're number three! We're number three!"

Because nothing about the game from the statistics to the outcome really counted, everyone involved seemed to feel that the game was pointless. Vince Lombardi called it "a hinky-dink game," but most people referred to it as the Losers' Bowl or the Toilet Bowl.

Officially at first, the game was known as the Bert Bell Benefit Bowl, in honor of the NFL's commissioner who had passed away in 1959. The name was switched to Playoff Bowl, but some referred to it as the Runner-Up Bowl.

Were players and coaches apathetic about the game? A *Sports Illustrated* story reported that five of the Playoff Bowls were tight ones while "five were blowouts—with an average margin of victory of 26.4 points per game."

Two-time All-Pro Roger Brown played hard throughout his five trips to the Playoff Bowl, winning each of those contests. However, even he saw the futility of it all. "I came in [third place] five times. That's garbage."

At best, players got a bit of a free vacation, but those who took along a wife may have wound up losing money on the deal as wives' expenses came out of players' pockets. Both the winners' and losers' shares amounted to a "bonus" of just a few hundred dollars.

WHAT WAS (ARGUABLY) ANOTHER POORLY CONCEIVED POSTSEASON GAME WHICH ULTIMATELY WAS DISCONTINUED AFTER BEING A SORT OF TRADITION FOR PORTIONS OF FIVE DECADES—A GAME WHICH ON ITS VERY SURFACE WAS A MISMATCH EVERY YEAR?

The contest was called the College All-Star Football Classic (also known as the Chicago Charities College All-Star Game), and it featured the reigning NFL champion against the previous season's top collegiate players—many of whom were destined for great things, but were, as mere youths, outclassed by the pros. One can easily imagine a grizzled veteran intimidating defensive tackle gazing across the line at a callow college player, snarling, "Welcome to my world, kid." While the pros were superior, winning 76 percent of the time, the College All-Stars did win nine of the 31 contests and managed to play to two ties.

The game was played from 1934 to 1976 with the exception of 1974 when NFL players were on strike. The event did prove to be a financial success from the start with the first matchup drawing 79,432 spectators.

The concept of the showcase game came from the same man, *Chicago Tribune* sports editor Arch Ward, who is credited with coming up with the idea of holding Major League Baseball's All-Star Games.

A University of Michigan player who appeared in the second game in this series went on to become the president of the United States, Gerald Ford. Another couple of interesting tidbits: It only took a few years for the college team to win, doing that in 1937, and in a bit of a shocker the college kids even managed to win in back-to-back years in 1946 and 1947.

FUTURE US PRESIDENT GERALD FORD PLAYED IN THE COLLEGE ALL-STAR FOOTBALL CLASSIC IN 1935.
(White House Photographic Office via Wikimedia Commons)

The NFL versus college clash was held each year at Soldier Field except for two years during World War II when the venue was changed to the home field of Northwestern University in nearby Evanston, Illinois.

The 1976 finale of this series was a memorable one, mostly due to some chaotic conditions. A downpour turned the Soldier Field surface into what could have served as a mud wrestling pit. The reigning champion Steelers were too much for the All-Stars, building up a 24–0 lead as the third quarter was winding down. When the winds kicked up and lightning was spotted, the referees instructed the teams to go to their locker rooms. At that point, many fans invaded the playing field, sliding through the muck. Police could not control the fans, some of whom tore down one of the goalposts. By that time, the field was reportedly under as much as 18 inches of water. An announcement followed, notifying the crowd that the game was called off, which prompted more unruliness and fistfights. That game marks the last time an NFL squad played against any team that was not a member of the NFL.

As the series had neared its end, several factors ensured the death of the showcase game. NFL coaches, for instance, were unhappy that their draft picks were being exposed to the possibility of serious injuries in a mere exhibition contest. The champion NFL team also naturally wanted to protect their valuable commodities. NFL coaches were also upset that some of their picks were missing valuable training camp time due to their involvement in the All-Star Classic.

Regardless, the series did achieve one purpose: It raised more than $4 million for charity from the 42 games played. The series also gave impetus to a tradition that began in 2004: the NFL Kickoff contest, which has the Super Bowl champs hosting a team for the initial game of each regular season.

CHAPTER THREE

THE GAME TODAY, THE 21ST CENTURY

The game of professional football has grown into gigantic proportions, secure in its place in the minds of millions as our national pastime. The players entertain with arguably more speed, quickness, strength, and savvy than ever before as each generation of the human race gets bigger, faster, and stronger.

This chapter is devoted to the game today, starting with the 2000 season and focusing on the players, coaches, games, and championships of recent years.

HOW MANY SUPER BOWL GAMES HAVEN'T BEEN SELLOUTS?

Only one, the first Super Bowl, which pitted the dynastic Green Bay Packers of the established NFL versus the upstart AFL's Kansas City Chiefs. Fans could casually stroll up to the ticket booth at the Los Angeles Memorial Coliseum and buy a ticket at game time, but even then, there was no walk-up rush that day. There were 61,946 fans who witnessed the 35–10 romp by the Packers in person back on January 15, 1967.

That may sound like a decent crowd, but the capacity of the Coliseum was a reported 100,594 (on one occasion an event drew more than 134,000 people to the venue), meaning there were more than 35,000 empty seats for the title game, a sight clearly caught on camera.

Ticket cost was an issue, but not the only one. The range of ticket prices was $6 for seats behind the end zones, to $10, and up to $12 for the best seats. Adjusted for inflation those three prices amount to almost exactly $50, a bit over $80, and nearly $100 by 2021. That aside, given the popularity and the frenzy surrounding the game in later years, the inability to sell out the showcase game still seems improbable, but it's true. Some suggest the NFL's decision to blackout the live broadcast of the game in Los Angeles upset fans who chose to stay home to display their displeasure.

HOW MUCH HAVE THE PRICES OF SUPER BOWL TICKETS GONE UP OVER THE YEARS?

Here is a sampling of ticket prices for the event over select years. The average price of a ticket for Super Bowl XII (held in January of 1978) was $30; for XVIII (1984) it had doubled to $60; just four years later, the cost hit $100; that amount quadrupled to $400 for Super Bowl XXXVI (2002); and it reached $800 for XLII (2008); Super Bowl XLVI tickets set fans back $900 on average in 2012. The Super Bowl held in February 2021, which was limited to an attendance of 24,835 due to COVID-19, cost spectators $950 for seats in upper corners and up to $3,600 for top-notch seats in spots on the lower levels of Raymond James Stadium in Tampa, Florida.

BY HOW MUCH HAVE ADVERTISING COSTS INCREASED SINCE THE FIRST SUPER BOWL BROADCAST IN 1967?

A 30-second commercial which aired during the first Super Bowl back on January 15, 1967, set advertisers back right around $42,000. The 2021 equivalent of that amount is almost precisely $350,000. The cost soared to $1.15 million by 1995 and topped $2 million by 2000. The price exceeded $5 million by 2017 and inched up from there.

Advertising costs during Super Bowl LV in 2020 were steep, with a half-minute ad running a new record of $5.6 million. Fox reaped huge profits, selling 77 national spots plus some local ads. Some companies paid a bit less because they purchased more than one spot, but every ad except one still sold for more than $5 million, for an estimated total of more than $400 million.

The first Super Bowl remains the only one that was broadcast by more than one network (NBC and CBS, the networks of the NFL and the old AFL), drawing 51.1 million viewers. The 2021 Super Bowl drew 96.4 million viewers, and that total was quite low—the lowest since the title game held in 2007. Thus, the Super Bowl held in 2021 continued a downward drop in viewership from the record high of 114.4 million who watched Super Bowl XLIX (February 2015) when New England topped Seattle. No matter what, the ads are astronomical.

WHICH QUARTERBACK, WHO SPENT ALMOST HIS ENTIRE 17-SEASON CAREER WITH HIS ORIGINAL TEAM, WAS THE FIRST QB TO TAKE TWO DIFFERENT TEAMS TO A SUPER BOWL, AND WHO WAS THE ONLY OTHER MAN TO DO THIS?

Peyton Manning, a Hall of Famer and a 14-time Pro Bowl honoree, was the first quarterback to take two different teams to the Super Bowl. In all, he guided his teams to four Super Bowls, winning one with the Indianapolis Colts, and, late in his career—in fact in his final season at the age of 39—one with the Denver Broncos.

The Pro Football Hall of Fame website states that, "His career began with a bang—starting all 16 games as a rookie and setting Colts and NFL rookie records for completions (326), attempts (575), yards (3,739) and TDs (26). His stats only improved from there."

His career was so long and illustrious, he managed to earn at least one win versus every one of the 32 NFL franchises now in existence.

To end the 2020 regular season, Tom Brady, who had already guided the New England Patriots to six Super Bowl victories, joined Manning, winning another championship with a second team. This time it was with the Tampa Bay Buccaneers, the team he had signed a two-year contract for $60 million with in March of 2020.

WHO WERE THE SHORTEST AND TALLEST PLAYERS IN THE NFL DURING THE 2021 SEASON?

As the season opened, the distinction of being the shortest NFL player was shared by four men who stood 5'6". Three are running backs: J. J. Taylor of the New England Patriots; Boston Scott of the Philadelphia Eagles; and Tarik Cohen from the Chicago Bears. The other man is a receiver/return specialist for the New Orleans Saints, Deonte Harty, who made First Team All-Pro as a returner in 2019 as a rookie (when he was known as Deonte Harris).

According to a story written by Max Molski for nbcsports .com, the tallest active players go 6'9". Baltimore Ravens offensive lineman Alejandro Villanueva is one of the men who stands 6'9". Dan Skipper, another offensive lineman who was active through 2020, was also listed at 6'9".

Molski wrote that "more than half of the teams in the NFL have at least one player who is 6'8". Patriots offensive tackle Trent Brown, Kansas City Chiefs offensive tackle Orlando Brown and even Villanueva's teammate Calais Campbell are among the most towering leviathans in the league."

WHO THREW THE MOST PASSES
IN A SINGLE NFL CONTEST?

Drew Bledsoe holds the record for most passes thrown in one game. On November 13, 1994, the Patriots quarterback, in just his second season in the league, heaved the ball 70 times (of his season total of 691 throws which led the NFL) against the Minnesota Vikings.

Down 20–0 in the second quarter, Bledsoe took to the air and New England rattled off 20 straight points to force the game into overtime. They wound up with a 26–20 win on a 14-yard pass from Bledsoe to Kevin Turner. Bledsoe ended the day going 45-for-70, good for 426 yards and three touchdowns.

On the year, Bledsoe was selected to the Pro Bowl for the first time as he led the NFL with 400 completions and with his 4,555 yards, good for 284.7 yards per game.

WHICH QUARTERBACKS HOLD THE TOP CAREER SPOTS FOR THE HIGHEST LIFETIME AVERAGE OF YARDS GAINED RUNNING? CLUE: FOUR OF THE BEST AVERAGES ARE OWNED BY MEN WHO PLAYED AT LEAST SOME OF THEIR CAREER DURING THE 2000–2020 TIME PERIOD, AND THREE OF THEM WERE QUARTERBACKS.

Michael Vick, who played for the Atlanta Falcons, Philadelphia Eagles, New York Jets, and Pittsburgh Steelers, has the highest average of yards gained per rush over a career at 7.0. For the record, the number two man on that list is quarterback Randall Cunningham, who played the majority of his career with the Eagles, at 6.4. Former Rams coach John Robinson once said of Cunningham's skills: "He's their leading passer, rusher and punter. Other than that, I don't know that he does a whole hell of a lot." It's no wonder he was sometimes called The Ultimate Weapon.

Robinson was correct about Cunningham, whose career average on punts stands at 44.7, and twice he boomed the longest punts of a given season, with one traveling 91 yards. His 1990 season with the Eagles vividly illustrates his versatility. Although he did not punt the ball once that season, naturally he did lead his team in passing with 3,466 yards and 30 touchdowns, and he actually was Philadelphia's top ground gainer with 942 yards, 257 more than his fullback, Heath Sherman.

Cunningham is followed by a big, barreling running Cleveland Browns back, Marion Motley, with his 5.7 lifetime average. Next comes the third quarterback on this list, the Seattle Seahawks' Russell Wilson (5.5).

WHICH QUARTERBACKS HAVE RUSHED FOR THE MOST LIFETIME YARDS?

Again, the majority of the top 10 leaders played at least a portion of their career from 2000 to 2020.

Once more, Michael Vick heads the list with 6,109. He is followed by: Cam Newton (5,628); Randall Cunningham (4,928); Russell Wilson (4,689); and Steve Young (4,239). Completing the top 10: Fran Tarkenton, Steve McNair, Charley Trippi, Donovan McNabb, and John Elway. The only men on the list from long ago eras are Tarkenton, who played from 1961 through 1978, and Trippi who goes back even longer, 1947–1955.

HOW IS THE STATISTIC KNOWN AS QUARTERBACK RATING CALCULATED?

Because of its complexity and how it weighs certain stats over others, the QBR is somewhat controversial.

In use since 1973 to evaluate quarterbacks' effectiveness, the rating is calculated by considering passing attempts, completions, yards, touchdowns, and interceptions. Under the NFL's formula, the highest possible passer rating is 158.3, and the lowest rating is 0. Critics have argued about having a highest possible score by saying, "Tell me the statistics for, say, a given game in which a quarterback could earn a perfect 158.3. Just (wildly) imagine he went 50-for-50 (in reality it had been very rare for a quarterback with the highest rating possible in a game to throw 30 or more passes). Imagine further that he threw for 600 yards, 12 touchdowns, and with no interceptions. A week later, a quarterback goes 51-for-51 for 601 yards, 13 touchdowns, and no picks. Doesn't he deserve at least a slightly higher rating than the first quarterback? How can there be an ultimate rating?"

That point aside, here's how the math works, but a word of caution—be prepared to get a severe headache or brace yourself to get ready to throw up your hands and say, "Just forget it!" The formula used combines "the values of four smaller formulas:

Formula 1: Take the completions/attempts, subtract .3 and multiply the result by 5.

Formula 2: Take the passing yards/attempts, subtract 3 and multiply the result by .25.

Formula 3: Take the touchdowns/attempts and multiply the result by 20.

Formula 4: Take 2.375 minus the result of interceptions/ attempts multiplied by 25."

But that's not all! "After calculating each of the four formulas, there is one final formula required to generate your passer rating: NFL Passer Rating = The sum of the results of Formula 1, Formula 2, Formula 3, and Formula 4 divided by 6. That result is then multiplied by 100."

By and large, most sports statistics are easy to figure out. Take a shot from the field in basketball and determining field goal percentage is a snap. Hit a grand slam? You now have four runs batted in. The quarterback rating system seems to require a degree in mathematics and/or a sturdy calculator.

WHICH QUARTERBACKS ARE AMONG THE HIGHEST RANKED WHEN IT COMES TO ALL-TIME, SINGLE-SEASON, AND SINGLE-GAME QUARTERBACK RATING?

Patrick Mahomes heads the lifetime list at 105.8. Other 21st-century quarterbacks also dominate this category. Deshaun Watson is ranked number two, tied with Aaron Rodgers and Russell Wilson, all above 100.

In the meantime, Green Bay's Aaron Rodgers is king for single-season rating, holding down the top spot (122.5 in 2011) and the second slot (121.5 in 2020). Peyton Manning follows with a 121.1 rating when he was with the Colts in 2004. Nick Foles, the only man to reach the 158.3 rating in a game in which he fired seven touchdowns, and Ryan Tannehill round out the top five.

Scoring a 158.3 in a game is referred to as the "perfect passer rating," and according to one source, this feat has taken place 78 times by 64 different players. The first man to accomplish this was Ray Mallouf in 1948 with the old Chicago Cardinals; and, through 2020, Tom Brady was the last quarterback to turn the trick. Eight men have racked up the 158.3 rating more than once, led by Pittsburgh's Ben Roethlisberger and Manning who each reached "perfection" four times. Kurt Warner and Brady did this on three occasions.

More trivia on the subject: Only three quarterbacks managed this feat as rookies, Drew Bledsoe, Robert Griffin III, and the only one to attain the score in his NFL debut, Marcus Mariota. In addition, four perfect ratings came in postseason contests, and three perfect performances came in losses, with Chad Pennington being the only perfect QB to play the entire game during a defeat.

Brady earned the distinction of being the oldest QB with a perfect passer rating when his Tampa Bay Buccaneers defeated the Lions on the day after Christmas in 2020. At the time, Brady was 43 years, four months, and 23 days old. He also became the quarterback who went the longest period of time between his first and final 158.3 rating, having gone a bit over 13 years between such games.

Tannehill holds the mark for the best completion percentage in a perfect game at 94.7, which again begs the question how was his game "perfect" when, for instance, he didn't complete every pass?

The fewest number of yards thrown in a perfect outing is 138 by the Atlanta Falcons' Scott Hunter in a 1976 game, and Bledsoe nearly matched him with his 143-yard performance in 1993.

In a way, though, the rating system has merit in that the list of Hall of Fame quarterbacks is dotted with men whose high ratings are at or near the top of the heap. Steve Young is number one at 96.81 followed by Peyton Manning at 96.5. Kurt Warner, Joe Montana, and Marc Bulger (not in the Hall) conclude the top four.

At the other end of the spectrum are the Hall of Fame quarterbacks who played that position long enough to throw 3,000 or more times. The ones with the lowest ratings are: George Blanda on the bottom at 60.6, Bobby Layne 63.4, Joe Namath at 65.5, and Terry Bradshaw checking in at 70.9.

Finally, believe it or not, 13 quarterbacks enjoyed a perfect rating, but also suffered through another game in which their rating worked out to a humiliating score of *zero*—and that list includes some real luminaries including both Peyton and Eli Manning, Otto Graham, Bob Griese, Dan Fouts, and Geno Smith, who had both the perfect rating game and the zero rating outing in the same season, 2014.

HOW RARE IS IT FOR A RECEIVER TO ACHIEVE A SORT OF TRIPLE CROWN, LEADING THE NFL IN TOTAL RECEPTIONS, YARDS GAINED ON THOSE CATCHES, AND TOUCHDOWNS SCORED VIA RECEIVING?

Going into the 2021 season this feat had been achieved a mere four times. Two Hall of Famers turned this "hat trick": Lance Alworth of the San Diego Chargers in 1966, and Jerry Rice in 1990 with the San Francisco 49ers. The other two men to accomplish this were Sterling Sharpe of the Green Bay Packers two years after Rice did it, and Steve Smith in 2005 when he was with the Carolina Panthers.

In 2021, Cooper Kupp of the Los Angeles Rams matched the feat of the other four stars when he hauled in 145 passes for 1,947 yards and 16 touchdowns. The 6'2" receiver out of eastern Washington also came awfully close to breaking the record for the most yards gained in a season on catches—he now stands number two on that list. That record belongs to Calvin Johnson when this Hall of Famer gained 1,964 yards on 122 receptions in 2012 to lead the NFL. Johnson scored only five touchdowns, so he fell far short of attaining a Triple Crown. Interestingly, the quarterback who threw to Johnson in his finest hour was Matthew Stafford, the same man who combined with Kupp in 2021 to threaten Johnson's record.

Trivia note: None of the men mentioned above are in the top 10 for the most catches in a season except for Kupp. The top position on that list is held down by Michael Thomas of the New Orleans Saints (149 in 2019). Kupp's 145 receptions shoved Marvin Harrison of the Indianapolis Colts out of the number two slot (143 in 2002).

To be fair to those who played when the NFL season was shorter, the top three receivers based on yards gained per game over a season are Wes Chandler (Chargers, 1982, 129.0 yards), Charley Hennigan (Oilers, 1961, 124.7), and Elroy "Crazy Legs" Hirsch (Rams, 1951, 124.6).

WHAT ARE SOME OF THE LARGEST AND SMALLEST NFL VENUES IN USE TODAY, AND WHICH WERE THE MOST EXPENSIVE ONES TO BUILD?

The New York Giants' home facility, MetLife Stadium housed in East Rutherford, New Jersey, holds 82,500 spectators to rank first in the league. Next comes Green Bay's Lambeau Field (81,441) followed by AT&T Stadium, home to the Dallas Cowboys and normally capable of holding 80,000 fans—but it can be reconfigured to hold 20,000+ more at times.

It's interesting that when it comes to large football venues, the NCAA far outdistances the NFL. The top three stadiums' capacities are the cavernous Michigan Stadium in Ann Arbor (107,601). Penn State's Beaver Stadium bulges at 106,572 capacity, and Ohio State plays their home games at Ohio Stadium in Columbus in a facility that can contain as many as 102,780 spectators. In all, there are seven stadiums with a capacity of 100,000 or more and seven more which exceed the capacity of MetLife.

The smallest NFL venues based on total seating are Chicago's Soldier Field at 61,500, and the home of the Arizona Cardinals, State Farm Stadium (63,400). Next comes a tie between Allegiant Stadium, home of the Las Vegas Raiders, and Detroit's Ford Field, both with a listed full house of 65,000.

IN THE NFL, METLIFE STADIUM IS NUMBER ONE WHEN IT COMES TO CAPACITY. (Anthony Quintano via Wikimedia Commons)

As far as the cost to build an NFL stadium goes, the Los Angeles Rams and Chargers share SoFi Stadium in Inglewood, California, which came with a price tag of $5.5 or $4.9 billion (sources vary). According to constructiondive.com, that facility cost more than double what the second most expensive stadium cost—and that even factors in an adjustment for inflation. Ranking behind SoFi is MetLife, which cost "roughly $2.03 billion."

The high price of such facilities is attributed to factors such as teams installing not only more seats, but larger ones as well. Teams also are coming up with "a larger number of boxes and suites." Another example is SoFi's double-sided scoreboard which "features more than 70,000 square feet of digital LED screens and weighs 2.4 million pounds, and had to be built to withstand earthquakes. . . ."

THROUGH 2021, WHICH STADIUM IS THE NEWEST AND WHICH IS THE OLDEST?

Two new venues opened their gates for the 2020 season. Allegiant Stadium in Paradise, Nevada, gave the Raiders an elegant facility, and in the short time since moving in, they've improved from the 7-9 record they had in 2019 to 10-7 in 2021. SoFi debuted in 2020 and the Chargers have also shown improvement, adding three wins each season since 2019. The Rams' first season in SoFi, which they share with the Chargers, was a success with the team winning in the wild card round before bowing out. They followed that up by winning the NFL West Division in 2021 and triumphing in Super Bowl LVI.

The oldest home to an NFL team is Lambeau Field, which dates back to 1957, although it has gone through some alterations since then. No other venue comes close to being that old—the next oldest ones began operation in the 1970s: Arrowhead Stadium, home of the Chiefs, and Highmark Stadium, where the Buffalo Bills roam. Of course, many facilities have had name changes over the years. The Bills' home field used to be called Rich Stadium, Ralph Wilson Stadium, New Era Field, and Bills Stadium.

WHAT IS THE RECORD FOR THE LARGEST CROWD EVER TO WITNESS A REGULAR-SEASON GAME AND A SUPER BOWL CONTEST?

Start with the largest crowd ever for *any* NFL game. In 1994, the Cowboys traveled to Mexico City to play the Houston Oilers in a preseason game, and a throng of 112,376 fans was on hand.

That aside, the regular-season attendance record stands at 105,121 for a game in which the Cowboys hosted the New York Giants at the spanking new Cowboys Stadium back in 2009.

Thanks to playing Super Bowl XIV (January 1980) in the spacious Rose Bowl, that game between the Rams and the Steelers drew 103,985 fans, with many of them rooting for their home market Rams. They went home disappointed as Pittsburgh won by a score of 31–19, on the strength of outscoring Los Angeles 14–0 in the final quarter.

HOW LONG IS THE NFL'S REGULAR SEASON NOW, AND HOW HAS THAT CHANGED OVER THE YEARS, AND WHEN DID THE CONCEPT OF A "BYE" WEEK ENTER INTO PLAY?

Before the 1935 season, pro football did not establish a maximum number of games to be played each season. However, the league did determine that each team had to play in a minimum amount of games. From 1935 to 1936 there was a 12-game schedule. From 1937 through 1946, the number of games played fluctuated between 10 and 11 games. Not long after World War II ended, stability set in with a 12-game schedule beginning in 1947. That expanded to 14 games from 1961 to 1977, then the schedule jumped to 16 until the 2021 season when a change pushed the season to its current 17 games over a period of 18 weeks.

The old AFL had a bye week built into its schedule when the league first began back in 1960. The bye week as we now know it started in 1990 when each team played 16 games over 17 weeks. However, there was actually one season prior to 1990—in 1966—when the NFL had an odd number of teams which required teams to occasionally take a week off.

WHAT IS THE LARGEST NUMBER OF EXHIBITION GAMES A TEAM USED TO PLAY, HOW DOES THAT COMPARE TO NOWADAYS, AND HOW DOES TODAY'S SHORTER EXHIBITION SCHEDULE AFFECT NFL COACHES' DECISIONS ON WHOM TO PLAY?

From 1961 through 1977, when teams played 14 games each season, each team also played in six or, at the very most, seven exhibition games. That, of course, is much different from today's game. Lately, four tune-up games has become the norm. In 2020, due to the COVID-19 pandemic, no exhibition games were held. In 2021, all NFL teams, with two exceptions, the Steelers and Cowboys who tipped off the season with the Hall of Fame Game, played just three such contests due to the expansion of the regular season to 17 games.

According to a *Sporting News* item by Jacob Camenker, the shorter exhibition schedule resulted in "minimal impact" because in recent years coaches were tending to sit their starters "for longer stretches of time." Camenker pointed out that the Rams' head coach, Sean McVay, decided in 2019 to use some of his starters in absolutely no preseason games. That included Jared Goff who was coming off a 13-3 record as the starting quarterback, running back Todd Gurley who had three 1,000+ yards rushing seasons under his belt, and Aaron Donald who was in the middle of a six-year run of being a First Team All-Pro defensive tackle.

Protecting key players from potential injuries was of paramount importance, but sitting starters also gives coaches time to look over "the back-end roster candidates." That's especially true because the official cut down date to 53 players on rosters comes rather late—August 31 in 2021.

WHAT ARE SOME OF THE FACTORS AFFECTING PLAYERS' SALARIES?

The current bargaining agreement in place for the NFL called for a 2021 minimum salary for incoming rookies to be $660,000. That amount was set to increase based on years of service, up to $1.075 million as the minimum for players with seven or more years of service.

Each season between the 2021 season and the time the current bargaining agreement ends in 2030, the minimum salary for first-year players all the way up to veterans with seven or more years of experience shoots up by $45,000. Thus, in 2030 every rookie must get $1.065 million at the very least, while players in the highest bracket must be paid $1.12 million or more.

The 2021 average salary per player is said to be more than $2 million a year, which is a bit misleading because many of the league's biggest stars, mainly quarterbacks, earn about $20 million annually, with the average salary for every single NFL quarterback pushing $6 million. In all, 34 players made at least $20 million in pay for the 2021 season, and sitting atop that list was a quarterback, Kansas City's Patrick Mahomes at $45 million.

For those with math skills, another way of looking at the money situation is to consider the median wage for every player in the league, and that was right around $860,000.

PATRICK MAHOMES WAS NUMBER ONE IN TERMS OF PLAYERS' SALARIES IN 2021. (Wikimedia Commons)

Next to quarterbacks, the position which boasts of the highest paychecks is defensive end. Those players have an average salary of $2.625 million. Surprisingly to many fans, running backs are among the lowest paid players, and they typically only last for about three years playing in the NFL. On average, a running back makes just over $1 million per season.

Tight end Tyrone Swoopes, a college quarterback who was first acquired by Seattle as an undrafted free agent, had an interesting but odd season in 2020. That year he made less money than any other NFL player, a mere $16,800. While he did sign a contract with Philadelphia in late August, the Eagles waived him before their opening game. He also signed on with Washington in December, but he never made it to the active roster. Therefore, he was considered to be a practice squad player who, under the NFL's collective bargaining agreement, did not qualify to earn the league minimum salary.

WHAT ARE SOME OF THE FACTORS AFFECTING SALARIES FOR NFL HEAD COACHES?

An ESPN story from December of 2021 made the point that the soaring salaries being paid to college head coaches "will force the NFL to adapt or get left behind." ESPN staff writer Bill Barnwell went on to state, "The old belief that an NFL head-coaching job is the pinnacle of the coaching profession might no longer be the case. . . ." One example mentioned of a prominent college coach was Brian Kelly, who had recently left his Notre Dame job to sign a deal with LSU worth $95 million over a 10-year span—with other incentives, his package deal was worth "north of nine figures." Then there was Mel Tucker, who was an assistant coach for the Jaguars, and who had also inked a contract (actually, a contract extension) calling for $95 million over 10 years to become the head man for Michigan State.

By way of comparison, although NFL coaches' salaries aren't usually known to the media, the low end of the salary spectrum is estimated to be around $4 to $5 million per year. On the high end, experienced big name NFL coaches earn around $10 to $15 million each season. Barnwell believes the highest paid coach of them all is New England's Bill Belichick whose earnings "could be as high as $25 million per year."

WHAT IS THE EARLIEST DATE AND THE LATEST DATE THAT THE SUPER BOWL HAS BEEN HELD?

Through the 2020 season, the Super Bowl held after that season's end was the latest one ever, with opening kickoff occurring on February 7, 2021. Then, starting for the 2021 season came a longer schedule than what had been played previously, a 17-game schedule over 18 weeks. That meant the Super Bowl was pushed back from the first Sunday in February to the second Sunday of that month. So, for now at least, the latest date for the championship game belongs to Super Bowl LVI which took place on February 13, 2022.

The first Super Bowl was held on January 15, 1967, but the earliest date ever for a Super Bowl contest was Oakland's 32–14 victory over Minnesota on January 9, 1977 (Super Bowl XI).

The last Super Bowl to be held in the month of January was the Buccaneers' 48–21 trouncing of the Raiders back on January 26, 2003 (Super Bowl XXXVII). The first one to be played in February actually came the year before. It was originally set to have been held in January, but was set back a week due to postponements having to do with 9/11.

HOW IMPORTANT IS HOME FIELD ADVANTAGE IN THE NFL TODAY?

In Major League Baseball, the home team wins roughly 55 percent of the time. That edge is a bigger factor in basketball than it is in any other major sport in America, with home teams winning almost 60 percent of their games and, from 1984 to 2019 in postseason competition, that winning percentage stood at 65 percent.

What may come as a bit of a shock to many is that the concept of a home field advantage in the NFL may, in fact, be a misconception of late. Based on the entire 2020 season, home teams had a slight *disadvantage* based upon their records. So, for what it's worth, here it is: Home teams actually posted a losing record that year at 127-128-1. That marked the first time ever that home teams experienced a cumulative losing record for an entire season in NFL play.

Even the year before, home teams sported a less than stellar record of 132-123-1, which had been the worst combined home teams' record since the start of the 16-game schedules which began in 1978. One report said that for many years experts routinely felt that playing at home was a comfortable advantage, a given that it was like starting a home game up by three points. But the home-field edge may be fading.

WHO PROVIDES THE GAME BALL IN THE NFL TODAY, AND WHO IS RESPONSIBLE FOR PROVIDING THE GAME BALL FOR COLLEGE CONTESTS?

Up until 2006, the home team in NFL play was in charge of providing all of the game balls for a given contest. In 2006, things changed when rules stated that each team was permitted to use its own footballs when they were on offense. Of course, the balls had to be checked by officials to make sure they fit specific NFL requirements—remember Deflategate—but that's another story for another day.

In college football games, the footballs used vary, but just a bit, from team to team. If a college program so chooses, it could, for example, use a ball that closely resembles the NFL's in size. A Wilson Sporting Goods director, Kevin Krysiak, stated, "As long as you fall within the rule specs, you have the ability to kind of customize and personalize based on your team's wants or desires."

So, college footballs can be personalized with, say, team colors or special graphics. For example, Ohio State University uses Wilson footballs, the "GST Prime" ball which features an Ohio State logo as well as "watermarked Buckeye images on the bottom half." That GST Prime football seems to be one favored by quite a few teams due to its "sewn-on stripes and Accurate Control Lacing composite leather laces," which are intended to give quarterbacks more grip points. "We do a lot of custom builds," Krysiak says, "trying to give the teams a little more personality."

WHAT IS THE PRIMARY DIFFERENCE BETWEEN THE FOOTBALL USED IN THE COLLEGE GAME AND IN THE PROS?

The football employed in college ball has two one-inch, white stripes painted halfway around the ball and placed about three inches from both ends of the ball, while the NFL ball has no stripes. Some receivers feel that the stripes make the college football easier to see and therefore easier to catch.

Other than that, there are minor differences such as college footballs *usually* being a bit smaller than the ones used in the NFL,

"THE DUKE"

even though both weigh 14–15 ounces and all of the footballs are made of leather. Most college footballs have polyurethane laces which are said to provide a better grip versus the NFL laces of extruded vinyl.

The college footballs are 10⅞ inches to 11⁷⁄₁₆ inches from tip to tip, while the NFL ball measures 11 to 11¼ inches. The circumference of the college football at the ball's widest point is 2¾ to 28½ inches. In the NFL it's 28 to 28½ inches long.

Even with the differences seeming to be minute, quarterback Chase Daniel, who broke into the NFL in 2010, has asserted that he can tell one football from the other even if he was blindfolded. He also believes the NFL ball can be spun somewhat better.

By the way, the NFL ball even has its own name, "The Duke," given to honor the one-time owner of the New York Giants, Wellington Mara, who was given that nickname by the Giants' players way back in 1925 when he served as the team's ball boy.

WHY IS THE FOOTBALL SHAPED THE WAY IT IS NOWADAYS?

First of all, footballs have not always looked as they do today. While it was never a perfect sphere like a basketball, at first footballs were much rounder than they are today, and they were about the size of a watermelon. That's a big reason why people used to employ the dropkick, but have now shelved that kicking method. Long ago, a player could drop the football and expect a pretty true bounce off the ground and to a good spot where he could aim his kick. Nowadays, a dropped football can result in a crazy, totally unpredictable bounce, hardly conducive for a dropkick.

Scientifically speaking, a football is called a prolate spheroid, and its shape can be traced back to the shape of an inflated bladder of a pig. The pig bladder, as mentioned earlier, is what the first footballs were made of. Eventually, footballs were made of cowhide and rubber and in 1934, they became more streamlined, more prolate and easier to pass and run with.

WHO GAINED MUCH ATTENTION WHEN, DESPITE THE SHAPE OF THE MODERN FOOTBALL, HE EMPLOYED A DROPKICK IN A GAME?

By rule, a dropkick must occur after the kicker drops the football and then makes contact with the ball just as, or right after, it touches the ground.

On New Year's Day of 2006, Doug Flutie's New England Patriots took on the Miami Dolphins in a meaningless game. The Patriots scored a touchdown and lined up in what seemed to be a formation for a two-point conversion. The 43-year-old Flutie backed up to the 13 yard line, puzzling the defense (and just about everyone else). He then caught the snap from center, took a few strides forward, then dropkicked the ball through the goalposts for the first successful dropkick since Ray "Scooter" McLean of the Bears did it in 1941.

McLean's kick came in the title game to help give Chicago the championship, 37–9, over the Giants. That dropkick proved to be the last point scored in the 1941 season. Strangely, by today's standards, in that championship contest the Bears four extra-point kicks came from four different men. Meanwhile, Flutie's memorable kick was the last time he'd be on the field during his 13-year career in the NFL.

WHICH KICKER REACHED 1,000 POINTS QUICKER THAN ANY OTHER PLACEKICKER EVER?

Justin Tucker accomplished this in just 118 games. He was also the first player to boot 30+ field goals in six different seasons. More impressive than that is the fact that he was the first NFL placekicker to be successful on kicks from the 20-, 30-, 40-, 50-, and 60-yard ranges in the same contest.

A member of the Pro Football Hall of Fame All-2010s team, this Baltimore Ravens star was a Pro Bowl selection in 2013, 2016, 2019, and 2020. However, through 2021, Tucker's most impressive accomplishment is his field goal accuracy rate of 91.1, which is tops in the history of the NFL.

HOW DID A DECISION MADE BY THEN PITTSBURGH STEELERS RUNNING BACK LE'VEON BELL WIND UP COSTING HIM MILLIONS OF DOLLARS?

Bell led the NFL in total touches in 2017 when he also topped the 1,200-yards rushing plateau for the third time. He then sat out the entire 2018 season due to a contract dispute with his Steelers.

That move cost him $14 million in salary for the season. In 2019, he did sign a four-year, $52.5 million (with $35 million guaranteed) contract with the New York Jets. That bundle of money got the Jets a paltry 867 yards over 17 total games from Bell.

Not only did he lose a ton of money by his less-than-shrewd decision to sit out a year, but after his productive 2017 season as a Steeler, he has never been the same. In 2019, as a member of the Jets, his average yards per carry was down nearly a full yard from 2017, and he ran for 502 fewer yards than he had in 2017. He then began to bounce around from team to team, running for a measly 328 yards in limited action in 2020, and getting cut by the Jets and later waived by the Baltimore Ravens. Late in the 2021 season, he did latch on to a job with the Tampa Bay Buccaneers. In his first game there he carried the ball twice for negative one yard. He ended his three-game stint there with eight rushes for 18 yards, giving him 101 yards for the season, less than what he averaged per single game in his finest season of 2016.

HOW HAVE TRENDS CHANGED REGARDING SOME OF THE EQUIPMENT PLAYERS CHOOSE TO WEAR?

As touched upon in Chapter One, the evolution of equipment has been remarkable. Aside from helmets, padding has changed the most throughout the years. Shoulder pads of the 1960s and into the next decade began to look rather large, and got even more cumbersome over the next 20 years or so. Roughly around the turn of the century the trend to small shoulder pads began. The position one plays is a factor, with players at the skill positions going with smaller, lighter, and, most importantly, less constricting shoulder pads than what is worn by, say, linemen who need more padding because they play in the violent world of their trenches.

Former college fullback Dale Stewart said that unlike the players of his era around 1960, many players today don't wear protection for some of their body parts. "Their knees are hanging out now, especially wide receivers. I think, 'Oh, boy, they're asking for it.' Running backs strip down to practically nothing because pads slow them down or hinder their mobility a bit. Some players basically wear just a helmet and shoulder pads." In previous years, players' outfits routinely included thigh, hip, and even rib pads, for example.

Stewart continued: "From 1951, when I graduated from high school, the changes are really wild. We had pants with hip pads built right into them. I think when I played service ball in the

JOHNNY UNITAS DISPLAYS THE
SHOULDER PADS THAT WERE IN VOGUE IN
1967 (LEFT). DEANGELO HALL AND ADAM
THIELEN SPORT THE MODERN VERSION.

(Wikimedia Commons [left] and Keith Allison via

Wikimedia Commons [below])

Air Force, you could slide the thigh pads into a pocket in the pants, but in high school all the pads were sewn into them, there was no pocket. So you had a helmet, shoulder pads, and the pants for protection. Long ago, even shoulder pads were sewn into the jerseys. They were not substantial at all.

"Now, even in high school the kids are really equipped. And in the pros, they have their pants cut up above the knees. A lot of wide outs are willing to give up padding for speed. But they're asking for trouble, because you are going to get hit.

"And if receivers or running backs wear hip pads, they're going to be much, much smaller than what was once considered normal. The shoulder pads vary—there are different shoulder pads for linemen, for running backs. There such a wide variety of equipment today, and the helmets aren't even close to what we had when I played."

Now, virtually every Division I team requires its linemen to wear knee braces and that's for practice sessions as well as, in many cases, games. This requirement even applies to players who have never had a knee injury.

Today's offensive linemen frequently wear a stabilizing elbow sleeve, something that didn't even exist decades ago. Likewise, compression arm sleeves are relatively new, and they do help muscles recover rather quickly, allowing blood to circulate to the heart faster than normal.

NFL players simply do not wear as much protection as they formerly did. They don't wear "butt pads" or hip pads, even though many high school and college players do. One source says the pros opt to go with fashion and how they look rather than focusing on safety. Hall of Fame running back Tony Dorsett was one such critic. "A lot of players dress to be in style, to look good on TV. . . . I was never like that. I would always dress like I was going to work—fully padded." He concluded, "I'm not all prettied up for TV."

WHAT IS THE NAME OF THE TEST THAT, UNTIL RECENTLY, WAS GIVEN TO NFL DRAFT PROSPECTS TO MEASURE THEIR GENERAL INTELLIGENCE?

Judging talent, potential, and even many intangibles of the players that teams are thinking about acquiring is vital. That is especially the case with prospective NFL quarterbacks. No team wants to draft a quarterback who *seems* to have all the right credentials, only to find out they've wasted a high pick on a bust.

There is a test which has been used by NFL teams to try to measure the future value of players. It's the Wonderlic Personnel Test, a valuable tool for NFL teams to judge players that was designed in 1936 by E. F. Wonderlic to try to determine the intellectual ability of people to function. In other words, it's like an I.Q. test which, for football purposes, gauges players' aptitude for problem solving.

The scores a player can earn run between one and 50 (the number of questions on the test), with a score of 10 indicating that the test taker is, at the least, literate. The average football player comes up with a score of around 20, while the norm for quarterbacks is right around 26. Teams look for quarterbacks who can score *at least* a 21.

Some of the scores by famous quarterbacks include: Aaron Rodgers who scored a 35, which placed him in the 96th percentile, which is to say he did better than 96 percent of everyone who took the test; Tom Brady's score was 33; Drew Brees and Peyton Manning scored 28.

The test is not, however, infallible. Carson Wentz has had his ups and downs. He had a win-loss record of 11-2 in 2017 when he was named the Player of the Year (winning the Bert Bell Award), but plunged to a 3-8-1 record three years later. His Wonderlic score? A whopping 40.

Then there's Heisman Trophy winner Johnny Manziel. The Cleveland Browns used a first-round selection to draft him in 2014, no doubt convinced he'd lead the team to better times than they had recently experienced (from 2008 through 2013, they lost either 11 or 12 games each season). Despite reportedly scoring a respectable 32 on the Wonderlic, instead of guiding Cleveland to the promised land, the so-called "Johnny Football" played in just 14 games over two seasons for Cleveland. He was given the starting nod in only eight games and had a 2-6 record to show for it.

The success of Patrick Mahomes, the 2018 MVP and Super Bowl champ whose score of 24 didn't exactly overwhelm coaches, has been well chronicled. A true winner, this man once threw 50 touchdowns in a season to lead the NFL. Plus, his record through 2021 when starting under center was 50-13, a success rate of almost precisely 80 percent.

Finally, there's Cam Newton and his score of 21, rather low, but few teams would have turned him away in his prime seasons. From the start he showed that he possessed the right stuff, being named the 2011 Offensive Rookie of the Year by the AP. Four years later, he still could dazzle, winning the AP NFL MVP Award after winning 15 games.

The highest score ever for this test was recorded by Pat McInally, who punted for the Cincinnati Bengals (1976 through 1985). He not only scored a perfect 50, but when he re-took the test, he came through with a score of 49. That prompted him to quip, "Missed one. Not a bad score after six concussions."

One source indicates the position which scores the highest on the Wonderlic is the offensive tackle spot, with an average score of 26. The lowest scores are turned in by halfbacks at 16 on average. Anyone can compare their knowledge with players by taking the test which is offered on line by websites including https://footballiqscore.com.

CHAPTER FOUR

MISCELLANEOUS WHO, WHAT, WHEN, WHERE, WHY, AND HOW

What follows are topics that don't fit neatly into the categories of the preceding four chapters.

WHAT IS A SCORIGAMI?

This term refers to a final score in an NFL contest which has never before been the outcome of a game. For example, in 2021, a Week 18 game ended with the Cowboys winning 51–26 over the Eagles. That was the 1,072nd time an unprecedented final score was registered in NFL play.

Jon Bois, an SB Nation writer, came up with the clever idea, and, thanks to social media, many followers have become interested in such occurrences. By the way, the Colts had also chalked up a Scorigami in Week 9 when they defeated the Jets, 45–30. For the record, there were 12 Scorigami outcomes in 2020 and half that many the following season.

As an aside, and speaking of odd scores, there have been just five NFL contests which featured a final score of 2–0. The last time this took place was way back in 1938, when the Bears squeaked by the Packers.

WHEN DID SACKS BECOME AN OFFICIAL NFL STATISTIC?

No official tracking of sacks took place until 1982, eight years after the man credited with coining that term, Deacon Jones, had retired. In 2013, the NFL began giving out the Deacon Jones Award each season to the player who led the league in sacks.

Looking back on Jones's playing days, footballreference .com lists his unofficial sack totals. The site credits Jones with five seasons leading the NFL in sacks over his 14-season career. His highest single-season sack totals are: 22 (twice), 21.5, 19, and 15. His lifetime total of sacks stands at 173.5, which ranks third among unofficial leaders. He trails Bruce Smith who had 200 sacks and Reggie White who got to the quarterback 198 times.

The record for the most sacks in a game belongs to Derrick Thomas of the Kansas City Chiefs, who took Seattle's quarterback down seven times in a 1990 contest. The most sacks in a season was 23 by defensive end Al "Bubba" Baker of the Lions, though that is an unofficial stat as he managed to do that in 1978. Officially, the top man in this realm is another defensive end, New York Giants Hall of Famer Michael Strahan with 22.5 over a 16-game schedule in 2001.

In 2021, Pittsburgh's T. J. Watt tied Strahan's record. Watt did play in a 17-game season when he tied the mark, but he was only in 15 games, one fewer than Strahan who played in all 16 of his team's games when he established the record.

HOW MANY KICKERS AND PUNTERS HAVE BEEN INDUCTED INTO THE PRO FOOTBALL HALL OF FAME?

Through the Class of 2021, there are 326 men who have been installed in the Hall, and the least represented position on the list is, by far, punters followed by kickers. As a matter of fact, Oakland standout Ray Guy is the only punter ever honored by the Hall of Fame. A mere total of four kickers are in, and two of them were on the field playing a position other than kicker most of the time: the ageless and peerless George Blanda and Cleveland Browns legend Lou "The Toe" Groza. Hall of Famers who were kickers exclusively were the Kansas City Chiefs' Jan Stenerud, and Morten Andersen, Mr. Automatic, the most recent addition to the Hall.

The most prolific kicker, Andersen, retired after a long, 25-year career which ran from 1982 to 2007, and he was inducted into the Hall of Fame in 2017. He scored 90+ points in 22 seasons, and went beyond the 100-point level 14 times. He wound up being the leading lifetime scorer for both the Saints and the Falcons. Andersen was the first man to blast three 50-yard field goals in the same game. He was so effective for so long, he was named to the All-Decade Teams of the 1980s and 1990s.

The Denmark native scored 2,544 points in all, ranking him behind only 24-year veteran Adam Vinatieri—who, with an all-time record 2,673 points to his credit is seen as a sure thing future Hall of Famer. He will first become eligible for Hall consideration in 2025. Vinatieri, in fact, ranks first for career field goals made, with a whopping 599, and second for points after touchdowns (874). It's no wonder this proud owner of four Super Bowl rings (earned with the Patriots and the Colts) made the NFL 100 All-Time Team. He became the first, and thus far only, man to score 1,000+ points for two different franchises. Vinatieri even holds the NFL record for the most consecutive field goals made with 44 from 2015 to 2016. His New England coach, Bill Belichick, called him "the greatest kicker of all-time."

Fred Cox, an all-time great placekicker, feels there should be more kickers in the Hall of Fame. He hung up his kicking shoes in 1977 yet remains the Minnesota Vikings all-time scoring leader.

Cox said of the lack of kickers' representation in the Hall, "I'm OK with it, because I understand what the situation is—it's really simple: most people don't consider kickers football players. It's a real irony when you consider kickers win, without question, more games than anybody else on the field. You either win or lose the game, but that's the way it is. Being that I'm a realist, a guy who was never expected to play pro football and to play for as long as I did, I learn to deal with that fact."

WHO WAS THE FIRST BLACK KICKER OR PUNTER IN NFL HISTORY, AND HOW MANY TOTAL BLACK KICKERS AND PUNTERS HAVE THERE BEEN IN THE LEAGUE?

Greg Coleman is recognized as the first Black punter in the NFL. He made history when he was drafted by the Cincinnati Bengals in 1976, but did not play an NFL game until he suited up for the Cleveland Browns. Coleman wound up playing the bulk of his career for the Vikings.

His cousin, major leaguer Vince Coleman, led his league in stolen bases six times in a row from his rookie season on. He stole an incredible 100 or more bases in each of his first three seasons.

Punter Reggie Roby followed Coleman, joining the Dolphins in 1983. The 16-year veteran went on to be named to the Pro Football Hall of Fame second team on the All-1980s squad. His trademark was punting the ball without taking a boosting jump, a rarity even now.

As of 2020, the last Black punter to play in the NFL had been Marquette King. He spent 2012 through 2018 with the Oakland Raiders and the Denver Broncos. However, in 2021, the Pittsburgh Steelers added Pressley Harvin III to the ranks of

Black punters. He handled kickoff duties and averaged 42.6 yards per punt. Harvin, who at 5'11" and a robust 260 pounds does not look like a prototypical punter, was the first Black man to win the Ray Guy Award (2020) as the best collegiate punter. He led the country with an average of 48 yards per punt that year.

Nevertheless, while Black athletes make up around 70 percent of all NFL players, it is, and has been, rare to see Black punters or placekickers. Harvin is only the sixth Black punter in NFL history.

As for Black placekickers, one report states that along with the first Black player at that position, Gene Mingo (1960–1970), there have only been four other Black placekickers. At the time of that report, since the NFL began there had been 1,418 roster slots available for kickers. The four men who have joined Mingo are Nigerian-born Donald Igwebuike and Obed Ariri, Justin Medlock, and Jonathan Brown.

WHO WAS THE FIRST KICKER TO COMPLETE AN ENTIRE REGULAR SEASON WITHOUT MISSING A POINT AFTER ATTEMPT OR A FIELD GOAL?

Gary Anderson, who played for five NFL teams and was a four-time Pro Bowl selection, went 59-for-59 on his PATs and clicked on all 35 of his field goal attempts at the age of 39. The South African kicker, who preferred to wear a one-bar facemask, achieved that feat in 1998 when his Minnesota Vikings set a record, since broken, for the most points scored in a season with 556.

Sadly for Anderson and his Vikings, he did miss a field goal after the regular season. In the 1998 NFC Championship Game versus the Atlanta Falcons, he missed a 38-yarder which gave hope to the Falcons. Sure enough, Atlanta stormed back (in a game which featured Minnesota's Anderson going against the Falcons' placekicker, Morten Andersen), forced the contest into overtime, and won the game, propelling them into the Super Bowl. For the record, Anderson's lifetime rate of field goal accuracy stands at 80.1 percent.

In 2003 there was a kicker who did Anderson one better: Mike Vanderjagt went through the whole season, including the playoffs, without missing any of his kicks. It should be noted that Vanderjagt did miss one field goal attempt, but in a game that didn't count, the Pro Bowl. It was there that he tried a 51-yarder in an effort to tie the game, but with three seconds left on the scoreboard, he finally missed. He would end his official streak during the 2004 season after 42 straight field goals made. As touched upon earlier, the record for consecutive successful field goal attempts, 44, belongs to another kicker with a last initial of "V," Adam Vinatieri.

By the way, and speaking of consistency, Stephen Gostkowski of the New England Patriots and the Tennessee Titans was the picture of perfection on extra points, setting an NFL record when he kicked 479 in a row—523 consecutive including postseason play. Over his 15 seasons, he missed 13 PATs, and in his second season in the league, 2007, he led the league, making all 74 of his extra-point attempts. Through 2020 he also ranked higher than anyone for averaging the most points per game played over an NFL career.

STEPHEN GOSTKOWSKI KICKING
FOR THE PATRIOTS
(Keith Allison via Wikimedia Commons)

WHO IS CREDITED AS BEING THE FIRST TO KICK SOCCER STYLE IN THE NFL?

As far as the NFL goes, the first soccer-style kicker was Pete Gogolak, but the man who is said to have first introduced soccer-style kicking to the game of football is Fred Bednarski. On October 19, 1957, the University of Texas walk-on who had already "sent kickoffs high and deep," lined up to attempt a 40-yard field goal. The Longhorns opponent, the Arkansas Razorbacks, saw him take his spot on the field and immediately thought something was up. They suspected a fake kick, judging from Bednarski's unusual positioning, far behind the ball and his holder, and about 5 yards diagonally, off to the side of the holder. Instead of running a trick play, he kicked what was then the third longest field goal in conference history.

Cox noted, "You can actually kick a soccer ball further than you can kick a football. Even when I was in high school, I could kick a soccer ball 80 yards." It didn't take coaches long to realize that the soccer-style kicker could boom a football a whole lot farther than the straight-on kickers could.

WHAT NOTRE DAME DEFEAT IS ONE OF THE MOST STARTLING LOSSES IN THE HISTORY OF COLLEGE FOOTBALL?

Given that it's impossible to pick the biggest upset victory ever, here's a handpicked stunner that is certainly one of the wildest and most interesting upsets ever.

In November of 1926, Carnegie Tech (now known as Carnegie Mellon University) engineered one of the most eye-popping upsets in the long history of college football. Hosting the legendary Knute Rockne's undefeated Notre Dame squad was a daunting task for the Tartans. Not only were the Irish 8-0, they had surrendered a miserly seven points all year long. Tech had already lost two games—to Washington & Jefferson and New York University—but their defense was quite stingy with six shutouts already in the books.

Notre Dame needed wins over their final games versus the Tartans and an 8-1 University of Southern California team in order to be crowned the national champions. Rockne made the tragic mistake of looking past his current obstacle, unafraid of Tech. After all, over the last four seasons Notre Dame had manhandled the Tartans, winning all four games by a composite score of 111–19. With that in mind, Rockne opted to have an assistant coach work the Carnegie Tech game while he traveled to Chicago to watch the Army-Navy game.

The Tech game began with the Irish choosing to send many of their backup players onto Forbes Field's snowy surface. Soon, by the second quarter, the usual starters were in the game. Nevertheless, by halftime Notre Dame trailed, 13–0. Two second-half dropkicks by the Tech quarterback Howard Harpster, an All-American and College Football Hall of Famer, put the game on ice, 19–0.

Notre Dame's win over USC the following week meant little; Rockne was inconsolable. The next time he had to face the Tartans, in 1928 at South Bend, Indiana, Rockne again was burned by Carnegie Tech, this time by a lopsided score of 27–7. Not so astonishing this time as Tech enjoyed a 7-1 season that year to a 5-4 record for the Irish.

WHY WAS THERE ONCE AN NFL CHAMPIONSHIP GAME PLAYED ON A FIELD THAT WAS NOT 100 YARDS LONG—AND JUST HOW DID THAT WORK OUT?

That bizarre event took place in 1932, but before getting into that, some background information is needed. In 1930, an exhibition game was held in Chicago Stadium even though that facility housed a field which was only 60 yards long from one goal line to the other. The stadium's playing surface was also narrower than a normal field. In fact, the width of the field (45 yards) was so short "the sidelines butted up against the stands." Because of those conditions, special rules were drawn up and the game went off as planned.

Now, two years later, and just 10 years after the official inception of the NFL, the Chicago Bears and the Portsmouth Spartans finished their schedules tied for first place. That necessitated an NFL first, a one-game playoff to determine the championship. The teams were forced to play indoors due to a blizzard which had struck the very Windy City with the force of a Dick Butkus forearm blast. Forced to act quickly, the site chosen for the all-important game was Chicago Stadium.

It was decided to use the same ground rules which had been applied to the previous exhibition contest. For example, the teams were required to kick off from the 10 yard line. The officials pushed the team with the ball back 20 yards after they returned each kickoff, and another 20 yards after they crossed midfield. Those moves were designed to make up for the 40-yard shortage of the field, thus requiring each team to, in effect, travel a full 100 yards' worth of turf for a touchdown. A punt which went out of the end zone meant the receiving team would take over at the 15 yard line; and if a punt hit a rafter, it was called a touchback, which also gave the receiving team the ball on their own 15 yard line.

Defense was the name of the game with the Bears winning 9–0 in a game which featured only one returned punt. One kick was even said to have sailed wildly and struck the organist.

One unpleasant sort of side effect of playing at Chicago Stadium was the fact that a circus had been held there one week earlier. After the circus had left town, elephant manure was left behind, and its odor reportedly caused one (human) Bear to throw up on the field.

WHO ARE SOME OF THE MEN WHO PLAYED PROFESSIONALLY IN BOTH PRO BASEBALL AND FOOTBALL?

In addition to the previously discussed Jim Thorpe, a select list of such multitalented athletes includes these men who played football and big-league baseball: George "Papa Bear" Halas; Washington Redskins halfback Vic Janowicz; Ernie Nevers, who set a record (later tied by Dub Jones and Gale Sayers as a rookie) when he scored six touchdowns in a game; Bo Jackson, a dynamo of a running back for the Raiders from 1987 to 1990 who was of Pro Bowl caliber and was also an All-Star in baseball; Atlanta Falcon defensive back Brian Jordan (1989–1991); and Hall of Fame defensive back and occasional receiver Deion Sanders who played on five teams (1989–2000 and 2004–2005).

Halas was such a fine football player in the 1920s he was named to the Hall of Fame's All-1920s Team. He was such a tremendous coach, he was the Associated Press (AP) pick as the Coach of the Year twice, not to mention his six NFL championships over his 40-year coaching career. As a big leaguer, he only played one season, 1919. In fact, he only played in 12 games and only managed to hit .091 with just two hits to his credit.

However, he mistakenly became a part of baseball trivia when some sources stated that Halas held down the right field position for the New York Yankees immediately before Babe Ruth did.

Halas did cover ground in Ruth's primary right field position, but in just five contests, and he played in his last baseball game on July 5, 1919, long before Ruth played in his first game as a Yankee on April 14, 1920. The man who deserves credit as mainly holding down Ruth's position before he took over is Sammy Vick. Nevertheless, it remains true that Halas is the answer to the trivia question for being the player who was once struck out by Walter Johnson and later was once tackled by Jim Thorpe.

Janowicz's biggest claim to fame was his winning the Heisman Trophy in 1950. The Ohio State multiple-threat, multi-position player was just the third man to win that honor in his junior season. That year he played around 50 minutes per game as a tailback, safety, punter, and placekicker. In an 83–21 laugher over Iowa, he put 46 points on the scoreboard on six touchdowns, two on rushes and four by throwing TDs, and a Big Ten record 10 extra point kicks. In his two NFL seasons spent with Washington (1954 and 1955), he managed to score just 63 points more than what he had done in the one game versus the Hawkeyes. He spent 1953 and 1954 as a catcher and third baseman for the Pittsburgh Pirates, meaning he played both pro football and baseball in 1954. He found that drilling an opponent on the gridiron was easier than hitting a baseball, winding up with two career homers, 10 runs driven in, and a .214 batting average.

Jordan fared much better on the diamond, lasting 15 years, primarily with the St. Louis Cardinals and the Atlanta Braves. His personal highs included 25 homers, 115 RBI, and a .316 batting average.

Meanwhile, another Heisman winner (1985), Jackson, was a superb athlete, stoppable only by a nasty injury. An eight-year big league veteran, his best season came in 1989 when he crushed 32 home runs and drove home 105. So impressive was his power, other pros stopped and gawked when he launched mammoth

BEFORE BECOMING ONE OF THE NFL'S LEGENDARY COACHES,
GEORGE HALAS PLAYED PROFESSIONALLY IN TWO SPORTS.

(Wikimedia Commons)

home runs in batting practice. On the fields of the NFL, his career was meteoric, lasting just four seasons, but memorable ones at that. From 1987 through 1990, the Raiders rugged runner made it to a Pro Bowl, bolted for touchdowns of 88, 91, and 92 yards to lead the NFL for the longest run in three of his four years, and topped out with 950 yards rushing the year he averaged running for 86.4 yards per contest.

The most famous story about Sanders concerns the misconception about a day he played in both a Major League Baseball and an NFL game on the same day. He didn't, but he was in uniform for the two games in question. On October 11, 1992, he played in a game for the Falcons in Miami. It was arranged for him to be whisked away on a waiting helicopter after the game to an airport. From there, he flew to Pittsburgh to join his Atlanta Braves for a postseason game against the Pirates. However, he was never inserted into that game.

Several players such as Drew Henson (nine career at-bats with one hit) and D. J. Dozier (.191 batting average over 25 games) played in MLB and the NFL but made little impact in baseball.

Still other versatile players have been able to play in the NFL and to play pro baseball, but not at the major-league level. Several quick examples are Tim Tebow, who signed his first pro baseball contract with the New York Mets organization, Russell Wilson who played several minor-league seasons, and Kyler Murray, drafted by the Oakland A's.

WHAT WAS THE BIGGEST ANNIHILATION OF ONE COLLEGE TEAM BY ANOTHER?

As far as the college ranks go, on October 7, 1916, there was a farce of a game played between Georgia Tech and Cumberland University. The final score—no misprint here—was Georgia Tech 222 to 0 for Cumberland. The FanBuzz website reports that this game featured a kicker "catching his own kickoff for a touchdown." A Cumberland player, after taking the snap, decided he wanted no part of the football so he chucked it away and "immediately ran off the field in fear."

Tech, soon to capture the National Championship in 1917, was coached by John Heisman, who was also the college's baseball coach. Now, in the spring of 1916, Cumberland's baseball squad had defeated the Yellow Jackets by a 22–0 score, while using some ringers from the minor leagues. Months later, hellbent on revenge, Heisman cried havoc and let loose his stinging squad of football players, his "dogs of war," on the opposing Bulldogs.

In a way, the game never should have been played because Cumberland had dismantled its football program after the 1915 season, but Heisman threatened the school with a $3,000 forfeit fee if they didn't show for a game that had already been established on the teams' schedules.

Cumberland's baseball and football student/manager, a man named George Allen, had to quickly rustle up about 20 of his fraternity brothers to play—and most of them had no college playing experience. FanBuzz writer Patrick Pinak compared the slaughter to "a bunch of guys bringing toothpicks to a gunfight."

Statistics bear that out. Cumberland coughed up the ball 15 times, nine alone on fumbles. They were unable to make even a single first down. In the meantime, the Yellow Jackets scored 32 touchdowns—14 by air and 18 on the ground as they ran amok to the tune of 471 yards rushing. Cumberland ran for a negative 43 yards and did little better in the passing department, going 1-for-15 for 10 yards. Legendary sportswriter Grantland Rice chose to ignore the 10-yard completion for the sake of humor and hyperbole when he wrote that the Bulldogs best offensive play of the day was a fullback's run for a loss of a mere 6 yards. In truth, the only thing resembling a highlight was anticlimactic— on the last play of the game, Cumberland blocked an extra-point attempt.

The uninformed might wonder if Tech eased up in the second half. Only someone being snide would say yes and point out the Yellow Jackets led 126–0 at the half, scoring "only" 96 points thereafter.

To clarify how a player retrieved his own kickoff for a touchdown, here's how that oddity played out. Kicker Jim Preas hustled down the field, and when the Cumberland return man backpedaled then fell after bumping into the goalpost, Preas saw the ball ricochet off the return man's head. Preas then snared the ball for six points.

WHICH QUALITIES ARE MOST IMPORTANT FOR QUARTERBACKS LEADING LATE-GAME COMEBACKS?

Fred Cox said of his Minnesota teammate quarterback Fran Tarkenton, "Francis was a great guy, but he was a typical quarterback. He was good, and he knew it, and that's OK—I never had a problem with that."

Cox believed outstanding NFL quarterbacks require a healthy ego and, going hand-in-hand with that, a whole bunch of confidence. "You better be able to throw three interceptions in a game and know that your next pass is going to be a touchdown. That's just the way it is. If you don't have that kind of attitude in pro ball, you just can't play. You can't be worried about whether you're going to throw an interception. You're just not going to get it done."

Defensive back Andy Nelson was a teammate and friend of Johnny Unitas, the man he called "the coolest guy on the field. Nothing bothered him. He just never got rattled." No wonder Unitas owned 22 records upon leaving the game.

Even after winning the 1958 NFL championship in what has been labeled The Greatest Game Ever Played, Unitas, unlike so many of today's players, wasn't demonstrative. He knew he was good and, oozing confidence, he wasn't shocked he had pulled off the win. Nelson said, "John Unitas was a cool customer. Nothing excited him. He walked off the field after that game and he wasn't turning back flips or jumping up and down. His eyes were focused straight ahead. Like it was just another game. I thought, 'This man just played the greatest game of his life and it's like another game to him.' He just casually walked off. He took it all in stride.

"I rode home with him that night, and he never said two words. I got out of the car and he said, 'I'll see you tomorrow,' and that was it. It was as if he were saying so long to a buddy, leaving a factory after putting in an eight-hour shift." That was Unitas for you.

His belief in himself inspired teammates. Colts running back Tom Matte stated that Unitas was "the ultimate leader. You just looked at him and it was sort of like, 'God's speaking here.' We had great, great trust and belief in what he could do. He was expected to produce and he just expected the best out of himself."

Linebacker Myron Pottios added, "He was a smart quarterback, a cerebral type guy who would challenge you. He wanted to get you in a situation where he knew he could beat you." And, Unitas *always* believed he could, and would, beat everyone.

HOW DIFFICULT IS IT FOR ROOKIE QUARTERBACKS TO WIN IN THE NFL?

It can be very trying. Even some Hall of Famers struggled early on in their careers. Take Terry Bradshaw, who spent his entire 14-year career with the Pittsburgh Steelers, for example. While he did go on to earn four Super Bowl rings, the statistics from his rookie season were abysmal. He threw six touchdown passes, but four times as many picks, with 11 percent of his pass attempts winding up in the hands of the wrong team. Plus, those 24 league-leading interceptions came over just eight starts. His quarterback rating worked out to 30.4, hardly a positive omen. Rookie quarterbacks often take their lumps, and Bradshaw managed to win just three of his eight starts. His sophomore season featured 22 more interceptions, and his quarterback rating didn't climb above 64.1 until 1975, his sixth season in the NFL.

WHO WAS FOOTBALL'S VERSION OF JACKIE ROBINSON, A BLACK PLAYER WHO WAS A PIONEER AND WHO PAVED THE WAY FOR OTHER BLACK PLAYERS?

Well, the man believed to be the first Black professional player ever didn't exactly knock down doors for other Black players because while he, Charles Follis, did break into the pros, there was hardly a flood of Blacks to follow.

There were other early Black players in the pros, but by 1934 the owners of NFL teams had weeded them out, mainly it appears, through attrition. When the last Black player was gone, no others filled the void until after World War II.

Some early key names include Cleveland's Bill Willis, the second Black man to become a Hall of Famer, who played from 1946 through 1953, and Marion Motley, who also joined the Browns in 1946 and helped guide them to five championships in all. Motley became the third Black in the Hall. The first was defensive back Emlen Tunnell of the New York Giants, inducted in 1967.

It was another man, though, who gained recognition as the first Black player to actually sign an NFL contract, making him the pioneer who really opened the floodgates. This was halfback/defensive back Kenny Washington. The story goes that the Los

Angeles Rams had to segregate their team or they would not be permitted by law to lease the Los Angeles Coliseum. Washington was signed by the Rams in March of 1946, which was said to have infuriated many NFL team owners. That didn't stop the Rams from signing Woody Strode to a contract in early May of 1946.

Interestingly, Washington, Strode, and a true pioneer, none other than Jackie Robinson, were all teammates at UCLA. It's noteworthy that the NFL, by introducing men such as Washington to the league, actually had Black players on their fields one year before Robinson made his debut with the Brooklyn Dodgers. In 1946, Robinson was still in the minor leagues with the Montreal Royals.

Strode, by the way, would go on to enjoy a fine and long career in acting. Born in 1914, his first movie appearance came in 1941, and he continued acting into the 1990s. He had significant roles in *The Ten Commandments*, *Spartacus* (in a role which earned him a Golden Globes nomination), and *The Man Who Shot Liberty Valance*, starring Jimmy Stewart and John Wayne (who happened to be a college football player at the University of Southern California).

It wasn't until 1949 that a Black player was chosen in the NFL Draft, and that selection, George Taliaferro, didn't go until the 13th round. Only three of the 10 teams in the league signed at least one Black player before 1950, and most of the teams didn't have a Black player on their roster until 1952. Even then, the Redskins refused to join in on the integration movement—they held out until 1962. Their racist owner, George Preston Marshall, stated, "We'll start signing Negroes when the Harlem Globetrotters start signing whites."

WHO WAS THE FIRST BLACK QUARTERBACK TO TAKE HIS TEAM TO THE SUPER BOWL, AND WHO WAS THE FIRST TO WIN A SUPER BOWL?

Doug Williams is the answer to both questions. When the Washington Redskins won Super Bowl XXII in a breeze by a score of 42–10, they did so with Williams turning in a stellar showing. He won the game's MVP Award by throwing four touchdown passes, all in the second quarter. That set a new Super Bowl record for a half and tied the record for a Super Bowl game even though he needed only one quarter to accomplish his feat. He also threw for a record 340 yards and set a new mark for the longest Super Bowl touchdown pass of 80 yards—that despite the fact that he was just one day removed from a six-hour root canal procedure.

On Media Day prior to the game, one tongue-tied reporter asked him how long he had been a Black quarterback. Williams cleverly replied, "I've been a quarterback since high school, and I've been Black all my life."

WHO WERE THE FIRST NFL PLAYER, THE FIRST STAR, AND THE FIRST COACH OF HISPANIC HERITAGE?

Until the year 2000, it was believed that a fullback/punter named Jesse Rodriguez was the first Hispanic player (1929 Buffalo Bisons) in the NFL. However, further research revealed that Ignacio "Lou" Molinet beat Rodriguez to the punch by two years. The Cuban-born fullback played in nine games in 1927 for the Frankford Yellowjackets.

The first Hispanic-American star was running back Steve Van Buren, who thrilled Philadelphia Eagles fans from 1944 to 1951. Born in Honduras, he led the league in average yards gained on the ground per game in five straight seasons.

The next big Latino name to follow Van Buren is Tom Fears, the son of an American father and a Mexican mother who went on to play for the Los Angeles Rams from 1948 through 1956. A fantastic end, he was elected into the Hall of Fame in 1970.

Another star was fullback Ricardo Jose Casares, who went by Rick and who went to five Pro Bowl contests. His NFL career spanned 1955–1966, and his personal high in rushing was 1,126 to lead the NFL in his second season.

The first head coach with Hispanic roots was Fears, the first head coach of the New Orleans Saints. He didn't get a chance to shine there; saddled with an expansion club during his 1967–1970 tenure, his career record was 13-34-2.

A few other facts: Tom Flores was the first Latino head coach to win Super Bowls, doing so with his Raiders for the 1980 and 1983 seasons. He was also the first NFL Hispanic quarterback. He broke in with the Oakland Raiders of the AFL in 1960 when he led the league as a rookie for the best completion rate at 54 percent.

Van Buren was the first Hispanic to lead the league in a major statistical category when he rushed for 832 yards in 1945. Two years later he became the second man ever to reach the 1,000-yard rushing level at 1,008—and due to controversy concerning the first man to do this, Beattie Feathers, Van Buren may have, in fact, been the league's first 1,000-yard rusher. He was also the first Hispanic to enter the Hall of Fame.

Finally, the first Hispanic American to be the overall number one selection in the NFL Draft was quarterback Jim Plunkett, chosen by the Patriots out of Stanford.

WHO HAVE BEEN SOME OF THE TALLEST QUARTERBACKS OF ALL TIME?

Brock Osweiler played for three teams from 2012 through 2018, and, at 6'8" (according to nfl.com), he had no trouble seeing over the outstretched arms of opposing defensive linemen. He is tied with Dan McGwire, the brother of controversial baseball slugger Mark McGwire, as the tallest man to ever handle quarterback duties. McGwire was Seattle's first round choice in the 1991 NFL Draft, but he never quite panned out, going 2-3 as a starter.

Several other quarterbacks were listed at 6'7"—Paxton Lynch, who spent two years with the Denver Broncos (1-3 as a starter), and Mike Glennon, a rookie in 2013 who was still active in 2021 with the New York Giants.

WHO WERE SOME OF THE SHORTEST QUARTERBACKS AMONG MEN WHO HAD AT LEAST A FAIRLY LONG CAREER IN THE NFL?

An article by Joe Rivera for the *Sporting News* made the point that while they say in amusement parks, "You must be this tall to the rollercoaster," that's not exactly the case for NFL quarterbacks.

The shortest man of note ever to play that position is said to be Eddie LeBaron, nicknamed "The Little General." He was 5'9" (one source testifies he was only 5'7") and 168 pounds, but he lasted in the NFL from 1952 through 1963. He was voted to play in four Pro Bowl games despite owning a record as a starting quarterback of just 28-54-3, translating to almost exactly two defeats for every one of his wins. Being with the Cowboys in their first four miserable seasons didn't help his stats—in 1960, the first season of the Cowboys' existence, he led the NFL with 25 interceptions thrown. That season, Dallas went winless (0-11-1) with LeBaron being strapped with nine of those losses. With Washington earlier, though, his 59.3 percent completion rate was second best in the NFL, and he was the Redskins' punter for three seasons.

Next is Doug Flutie, who was two inches shy of the 6-foot level but went to one Pro Bowl and spent 13 years in the NFL.

In 1998, he finished third in the league with his 7.19 net yards per pass attempt. He's followed by Russell Wilson at 5'10⅝" and Sonny Jurgensen, a 5'11" Hall of Famer.

Of course, the height listed by teams has often been a literal and a figurative stretch. Some say Hall of Famer Fran Tarkenton, said to be 6 feet even, was a bit under that height. In any event, that didn't stop him from taking three teams to the Super Bowl.

Arizona's Kyler Murray, who is listed at 5'10⅛" (every fraction matters when one is as short as Murray) must feel as if he's playing in a world of giants and he's Jack. His passing and scrambling skills can bring many of those giants to their knees. When the Cardinals drafted him as the number one overall choice in 2019, he became the shortest quarterback to gain that distinction in the history of the NFL. Two years after being named the AP Offensive Rookie of the Year, Murray ranked sixth in the league with his 69.2 percent completion rate.

Finally, counting men who played in at least one NFL game, the shortest quarterback ever was a man who did just that—lasted only one game. A man named Jack Shapiro is, in fact, *the shortest man ever to suit up and see action in the NFL*. He was 5'1". His one game, which gave him a tie for the record for *the shortest* NFL career ever, came with the Staten Island Stapletons in 1929.

HOW DID THE SUPER BOWL COME TO HAVE THAT NAME?

The most commonly told version of the origin of that name is that the owner of the Kansas City Chiefs, Lamar Hunt, had children who had a toy, a very bouncy ball called a Super Ball. That gave him the idea to suggest Super Bowl for the name of the AFL versus the NFL championship game, and it stuck. Hunt himself said he came up with the name Super Bowl in the early fall of 1966.

However, this version has been refuted by some. The title game was originally named the AFL-NFL World Championship Game, and it would not get the title of Super Bowl until after the first three of those championship games were played—calling the first three title games Super Bowls I, II, and III was done retroactively.

There is some simple evidence to dismiss the Hunt story. Several weeks before the time Hunt claimed he used the term *Super Bowl*, the *New York Times* had already used that wording in print. That leaves experts to debate whether Hunt had the time period wrong concerning when he came up with the name or he is mistaken.

As a side trivia item, the use of roman numerals associated with the championship game did not come about until Super Bowl V.

HOW HAVE COLLEGE BOWL GAMES CHANGED OVER THE YEARS?

Long ago and for many years, there were just five bowl games played each season (and one All-Star Game, the East-West Shrine Game). All of the bowl games were held on New Year's Day. These biggies were the proverbial Granddaddy of Them All which dates back to 1902, the Rose Bowl, followed by the Sugar Bowl, Sun Bowl, and the Orange Bowl, which all began in 1935. Then came the Cotton Bowl Classic which began two years after that.

For the 2021 and into 2022 football season, a total of 43 bowl games were held between December 17 and January 10—and that's just Division I bowl contests, nor does that total count a handful of All-Star affairs.

Over the years, many bowl games have died out. A few of the now defunct bowl games include the Cherry Bowl, which drew 70,000+ spectators for its initial game yet had a life span of just two years, as opposed to the long-lived Bluebonnet Bowl which lasted from 1959 to 1987. The Gotham Bowl was another short-lived bowl—an attendance of right around 6,000 provided the mercy killing for this event in its second and final season.

There was also the Dixie Bowl and a Dixie Classic, a Freedom Bowl, an Oil Bowl, and a Poinsettia Bowl which was encumbered by having to bear the full name of the San Diego County Credit Union Poinsettia Bowl.

Some of the bowl games had rather odd, even amusing names. For example, Fresno, California, was host to the Raisin Bowl (1946–1949); there was a Silicon Valley Bowl held in San Jose State's Spartan Stadium; and the Salad Bowl in Phoenix which featured college teams from 1947 through 1952, then switched to featuring service teams and all-star squads. A few others: Cigar Bowl, Refrigerator Bowl, the Glass Bowl, and the first bowl game held outside of the United States—the Bacardi Bowl, also called the Rhumba Bowl, held in Cuba.

Of course, nowadays seemingly every bowl game has the name, no matter how absurd, of a sponsor tied in with the contest. Some sponsors even insist on adding their "dot com" after their name and before the bowl game's name.

WHICH TEAM, AMONG THE OLDEST OF ALL NFL FRANCHISES, WAS THE LAST ONE TO PRODUCE A 1,000-YARD RUSHER?

The Detroit Lions was the last team to finally have a runner who topped the 1,000-yard mark. That didn't occur until 1971 when fullback Steve Owens romped for 1,035 yards (number four in the league, less than 100 yards behind leader Floyd Little) in his first full NFL season. His Lions franchise dates back to 1930 (when they were the Portsmouth Spartans), so it took 41 years for them to come up with a 1,000-yard rusher.

The Washington Redskins (who began play long ago as the Boston Braves) and the New York Giants took nearly as long as Detroit with their first 1,000-yard rushers coming along just one year before the Lions achieved this. In 1970, Larry Brown accumulated 1,125 yards rushing while averaging 4.7 yards per carry. Curiously, he scored just five touchdowns that season.

Meanwhile, in 1970, Ron Johnson became the first Giants runner to reach the 1,000-yard plateau with his 1,082 yards. He only averaged 3.9 yards a carry but did score eight times. It actually took the Giants longer to have a man rush for 1,000 yards than Detroit because the New York franchise dates back five years farther than the Lions. By the way, Johnson had a brother, Alex, who played in the major leagues from 1964 through 1976, and who led the American League in hitting in 1970 when he hit .329 for the California Angels.

WHO IS THE FIRST QUARTERBACK TO RUSH FOR 1,000 OR MORE YARDS IN A SINGLE SEASON?

Bobby Douglass of the Chicago Bears came oh so close to being the first quarterback to take off and run for 1,000 yards. In 1972, he amassed 968 yards on the ground (number 11 in the league) to break a 34-year-old record. Amazingly, Douglass not only had enough rushing attempts to qualify for the league lead among NFL runners, he did top the league for average yards per carry at 6.9, almost a yard and a half more than the number two man on the list, Pittsburgh Steelers Hall of Famer Franco Harris (at 5.6). Douglass even ripped off the sixth-longest run of the year when he scampered 57 yards that season.

Douglass's record high stood until 2006 when Atlanta's Michael Vick broke the 1,000-yard barrier when he dashed for 1,039, although it should be noted he broke the old record by playing over a 16-game schedule versus the 14-game schedule Douglass played. Still, Vick did average an incredible 8.4 yards per carry—tied with running back Beattie Feathers for the top mark of all time—and Vick led the NFL in that category five times. Incidentally, another great running quarterback, Randall Cunningham, averaged 8.0 yards per carry in 1990 as a member of the Philadelphia Eagles to hold down the number three position in this department.

Final note on Douglass: Bill Veeck, who was the owner of the Chicago White Sox when Douglass was in Chicago with the Bears, signed the strong-armed Douglass to a minor-league contract as a pitcher. Then 32 years old, Douglass began at a high level, Triple-A ball, long before Michael Jordan played Double-A minor-league baseball in the White Sox organization. The Douglass experiment failed quickly, after four relief appearances. He walked 13 batters and struck out none because, as writer Al Yellon put it, "No one could hit him because he couldn't throw strikes . . . in baseball as in the NFL, not hitting his target [was his problem]." How true: He threw 36 career touchdown passes while generously throwing 64 interceptions.

WHO NOW IS THE RECORD HOLDER FOR THE MOST YARDS RUSHED IN A SINGLE SEASON BY A QUARTERBACK; AND HAS ANY QUARTERBACK'S TOTAL BEEN HIGH ENOUGH THAT HE LED HIS TEAM IN RUSHING AS WELL?

After Michael Vick ran for his 1,039 yards in 2006, Lamar Jackson of the Baltimore Ravens capered for 1,206 yards in 2019 (6.9 per carry). That year, he was named the Offensive Player of the Week five times to tie the record he now shares with Cam Newton and Tom Brady (who also holds the record for being the Offensive Player of the Week 31 times over his career through 2020).

Gazing back 50 years from 1970 through 2019, there have been seven quarterbacks who led their team in rushing. The illustrious list: Bobby Douglass, Randall Cunningham, Donovan McNabb, Newton, Russell Wilson, Josh Allen, along with a not so distinguished entry—in 2019 Ryan Fitzpatrick did lead his Dolphins in rushing, but with a meager total of 243 yards. Newton and Jackson both twice led their team, while Cunningham did this rare feat four times (three times with a total fewer than 625 yards).

WHO ARE SOME OF THE MOST NOTABLE LEFT-HANDED-THROWING QUARTERBACKS EVER?

Bobby Douglass was the Bears' quarterback from 1969 through a small portion of the 1975 season. An article on chicago.sbnation.com states, "At the time he was drafted, a left-handed quarterback was viewed like a left-handed catcher in baseball would be—a freak, a rarity." Only four lefties had ever played the key position in the annals of the NFL up until Douglass came along, and only one was really rather famous, Allie Sherman.

However, although Douglass was a sort of pioneer, he was not a very good quarterback. His lifetime record as a starting quarterback was a pathetic 16-36-1, meaning he only won 30 percent of his starts.

Probably the most famous left-handed quarterbacks soon to follow Douglass were Boomer Esiason, Ken Stabler, and then Steve Young, but there have been others of note such as Jim Zorn and Frankie Albert.

More recently the list has to include men such as Mark Brunell, who played for a number of NFL teams and was a member of the New Orleans Saints when they won Super Bowl XLIV in 2010. In addition, Michael Vick lasted 13 seasons (2001–2015), mainly with the Atlanta Falcons and the Philadelphia Eagles. In 2021, Tua Tagovailoa joined the ranks of southpaw quarterbacks

LEFTY MICHAEL VICK PASSING FOR THE ATLANTA FALCONS (WIKIMEDIA COMMONS)

when he left the campus of the University of Alabama and was a first-round choice of the Miami Dolphins.

Tim Tebow didn't last long in the NFL (2010–2012), but he did win the Heisman Trophy in 2007, making him the first sophomore ever to take that prestigious honor. A few others who didn't make a huge impact as an NFL lefty QB: Kellen Moore; Chris Simms, son of Phil, the New York Giants' two-time Super Bowl winner; two USC products in 2004 Heisman winner Matt Leinart and Paul McDonald; Tyler Palko; and 1962 Heisman winner Terry Baker who played in the NFL and the Canadian Football League.

HAS THERE EVER BEEN A LEFT-HANDED QUARTERBACK WHOSE STARTING CENTER WAS ALSO LEFT-HANDED?

For the bulk of southpaw Jim Zorn's career with Seattle (1976–1984), the Seahawks had a left-handed center in John Yarno. The odds of two lefties working together as the man under center and his snapper are slim, but what are the odds of a center with the last initial of "Y" hiking the ball to a fellow lefty with the last initial of "Z"? People often speak of an A-to-Z range, but here was an unheard of Y-Z duo.

Zorn was stuck with some not-so-good Seattle teams. In fact, his rookie season was also the inaugural season for the Seahawks franchise, but in his second season in the league he led the NFL with an average of 16.2 yards for each of his completions. Many of Zorn's completions went to his favorite target, Hall of Fame wide receiver Steve Largent, like Yarno, a fourth-round acquisition.

Yarno was the 87th pick overall in the 1977 Draft, and he stuck around for six seasons, the last five as the team's starting center. He had been a First Team All-American for the Idaho Vandals (1976) where he would have his jersey number retired. After his days in the NFL, he and his brother George signed on with the Denver Gold of the United States Football League.

WHICH COLLEGES HAVE PRODUCED THE MOST NFL HALL OF FAMERS AS OF 2021?

A tie for the top spot exists between the University of Southern California and its rival Notre Dame. They've both churned out 13 Pro Football Hall of Famers. They include Marcus Allen, Frank Gifford, Ronnie Lott, and Troy Polamalu out of USC and, from the Fighting Irish luminaries Joe Montana, Tim Brown, and Paul Hornung.

Next on the list is the University of Michigan with 11; Ohio State at 10; then the University of Miami and Pitt with nine each.

WHICH SOMEWHAT OBSCURE RUNNING BACK NOT ONLY LED THE NFL IN RUSHING IN 1952, BUT STILL HAS ONE OF THE MOST IMPRESSIVE RESUMES FOR A MAN WHO HAS YET TO BE INDUCTED INTO THE PRO FOOTBALL HALL OF FAME?

"Deacon" Dan Towler hailed from the same small town, Donora, Pennsylvania, which produced Hall of Famers Stan "The Man" Musial and Ken Griffey Sr. and son Griffey Jr. Towler led the NFL in rushing in 1952, and was in four Pro Bowls over his career of five full seasons. When an all-time Rams team was chosen once, the running backs were Eric Dickerson and Towler.

Only five running backs own a higher single-season average per carry than Towler's 6.8 from 1951. His 5.2 yards per rush lifetime is better than what Gale Sayers produced (5.0) and matches exactly the output of Jim Brown. He led the NFL for the most rushing touchdowns two times. Towler even scored more career touchdowns than Sayers, 43–39, and yet another Hall of Famer, Floyd Little.

Hall of Famer Raymond Berry called Towler "a man who our Colts defensive players thought the world of . . . . They said he was one of the toughest guys to tackle that they ever had to face." Not bad for a man who was the 324th overall pick (25th round) in the draft.

According to the website deacondantowler.com, Towler deserves Hall of Fame status and it quotes Joe Montana as agreeing, saying, "He is deserving and his time has come to be recognized as one of the greats in our game of professional football."

Army All-American quarterback Arnold "Pope" Galiffa was another athletic standout from Donora. Someone joked that the town must have been a highly religious one as it produced, a Deacon, a Pope, and, in Musial, a [St. Louis] Cardinal.

WHAT ARE SOME OF THE BEST NICKNAMES THAT HAVE BEEN ATTACHED TO CERTAIN TEAMS OF GIVEN ERAS, OFTEN TO CELEBRATE SOME EXCEPTIONAL TALENT OF THE TEAM SUCH AS ITS STAUNCH DEFENSE?

Some select names in this not all-inclusive list are:

- The Monsters of the Midway, a colorful moniker given to the Chicago Bears team dating back to the early 1940s. The Bears of 1985 with Mike Singletary and Richard Dent and the 2006 Bears with men such as Brian Urlacher were so intimidating that the Monsters nickname came out of mothballs to be applied to them as well.

- The Steel Curtain defense of the Pittsburgh Steelers from the 1970s time period included Hall of Famers such as Jack Ham, "Mean Joe" Greene, Jack Lambert, Mel Blount, and Donnie Shell. The Steelers defense circa the mid-1990s also earned a nickname, Blitzburgh.

- The Fearsome Foursome of the Los Angeles Rams was so potent and enduring, the nickname stuck around from parts of the 1960s and into the next decade. The original quartet was Deacon Jones and Merlin Olsen, both Hall of Famers, along with Lamar Lundy, and Rosey Grier. In 1967, Grier was gone, replaced by Roger Brown who in turn was replaced by Diron Talbert in 1970. That year Coy Bacon replaced Lundy. It should be noted that before the Rams foursome, the Giants, Chargers, and Lions also had groups of studs with that same nickname.

- The Purple People Eaters refers to the Minnesota Vikings defensive line of the 1970s which featured two future Hall of Famers, Carl Eller and Alan Page, as well as Jim Marshall and Gary Larsen. Furthermore, those men are the only front four to go to the Pro Bowl together, with all of them selected to the squad in 1969.

- In the 1970s, the Cowboys defense was so feared they were called the Doomsday Defense (with two renditions of the unit). Stars included Bob Lilly, Mel Renfro, and for the Doomsday II version, Randy White and Ed "Too Tall" Jones.

- The Orange Crush was a name the Denver Broncos went by when they had defensive stalwarts Tom Jackson, Randy Gradishar, and Lyle Alzado in the 1970s.

- Thanks to a popular musical group, Gloria Estefan's Miami Sound Machine of the late 1980s, the Dolphins defense was dubbed the Miami Pound Machine. Previously, there was Miami's No-Name Defense. In 1972, those men who toiled in relative anonymity, produced the NFL's only undefeated Super Bowl champs with their 17-0 squad.

- The Hogs was a nickname given this time to an offensive unit, Washington's offensive line (plus honorary hog fullback John Riggins) of the 1980s. It was made up of behemoths

including Russ Grimm, Mark May, and Joe Jacoby, who
unleashed runners such as Riggins.

- Of course another Washington team of the early 1970s
had their own colorful nickname, the Over-the-Hill Gang.
That crew was made up of many aging, but still talented,
veterans—the average age of their starting players was 31.
Head coach George Allen, spouting the line, "The future is
now," traded seven draft picks for men (many coming from
the Rams, the team he had coached in 1970) such as linebackers Myron Pottios and Jack Pardee.

- The Big Blue Wrecking Crew and Big Blue were nicknames attached to the New York Giants defensive units from
around 1986 to 1990. Those teams won two Super Bowls
led by Lawrence Taylor. Earlier, the Giants had their Crunch
Bunch featuring the league's top linebackers in Brad Van
Pelt, Harry Carson, as well as Brian Kelley and Taylor.

- The 1999 St. Louis Rams offense earned the moniker of
the Greatest Show on Turf thanks to their record-setting
ways. That team won the Super Bowl thanks to high-octane
offensive players such as Marshall Faulk, Torry Holt, Isaac
Bruce, and Kurt Warner. The Rams had their own Mob
Squad starting in 2015, as personified by defensive tackle
Aaron Donald.

- The Seattle Seahawks' smothering secondary of the
2010s era became known as the Legion of Boom. That
group began with Earl Thomas, Kam Chancellor, Richard
Sherman, and Brandon Browner. After a while, the nickname was applied to their entire defense. From 2012
through 2015, Seattle led the NFL in permitting the fewest
points each year, something only the Cleveland Browns had
done in the 1950s.

- The San Diego Chargers were once known as the team with the Air Coryell offense, named after the team's let-the-ball-fly head coach Don Coryell. With Dan Fouts at quarterback, the second man to throw for more than 4,000 yards, this offense was as explosive as nitro.

Some other team nicknames in no special order: San Diego's groups of the Bruise Brothers and the Border Patrol; the Miami Dolphins' Killer Bees swarming defense; the Houston Texans' defense, the Bulls on Parade; the Atlanta Falcons' nickname of the Dirty Birds began during the season the Falcons, who punctuated their scores with an electrifying celebratory end zone dance, were headed to their first Super Bowl appearance at the end of the 1998 season; Washington boasted of a defensive line called the Department of Defense starting in 2020; O. J. Simpson, aka Juice, benefited from running behind a group of men called the Electric Company, men who "turned on the Juice" who ran for 2,003 yards in 1973. The biggest name player of that O-line was Reggie McKenzie, but a rookie guard named Joe DeLamielleure was then at the start of a Hall of Fame career.

A trio of Bronco wide receivers even had their own nickname, the Three Amigos. In the late 1980s this group was made up of Vance Johnson, Mark Jackson, and Ricky Nattiel.

Finally, a derisive nickname. By the time the New Orleans Saints had lost the first 14 games of their 1980 season, a local sportscaster had stirred things up, encouraging his listeners to wear paper bags over their heads at home games. Anonymity for those attending games of the embarrassing Saints was important, and many fans took to calling the team the Aints, a far cry from the Who Dat Nation name given to ardent Saints fans of late.

WHAT ARE SOME OF THE BEST NICKNAMES FOR NFL PLAYERS?

The list is so long, a small sample has to suffice here. A handful of men who played in relatively recent years includes the bruising Jerome Bettis who was "The Bus"; Calvin Johnson went by "Megatron"; Marshawn Lynch earned the intimidating nickname of "Beast Mode"; and Tyrann Mathieu answered to "Honey Badger."

Dipping back to players from various parts of the 20th century: Craig Heyward was "Iron Head"; Reggie White, who did become an ordained Baptist minister was called "The Minister of Defense" (and sometimes "Big Dawg"); and there was another man who became a minister after leaving the NFL, "Deacon" Dan Towler. John Cole's nickname, naturally, was "King." Gene Lipscomb was much better known as "Big Daddy" due to what was considered to be in his era a huge 6'6", 284-pound frame. Emlen Tunnell was poetically known as "The Gremlin" just as Tom Tracy was "Tom the Bomb" and George Karamatic was "Automatic."

There was a "Tarzan" Taylor and a "Tarzan" White. Byron "Whizzer" White made an enormous, quick impression in the pros, leading the NFL in rushing, total carries, yards gained per game played, and the longest run of the season in his rookie season (1938). He led again in rushing the next year, but quit football after his third season.

Harold Grange had three nicknames: mainly going by "Red," he was also called "The Galloping Ghost" and, on occasion, "The Wheaton Iceman," coming from a summer job he held and the name of the town where he attended high school (and scored 75 touchdowns), Wheaton, Illinois. Tony Canadeo had a very wordy nickname, which was similar to Grange's, going by "The Gray Ghost of Gonzaga" (his college).

Powerful nicknames abound: Randy White went by "The Manster" (half man, half monster), Larry Craig was called "Superman," and Dave Smukler was sometimes called "Dynamite" because of his durability. He went his entire 11-season career without missing a game, setting a record which lasted for 13 years with his 121 straight games played, and he played both ways, sometimes logging 60 minutes in games.

A year after he died fighting in World War II, Al Blozis was given the nickname of "The Human Howitzer" in a comic book which featured a story about his life. In 1944, while home on furlough from the Army, he substituted his military uniform for his New York Giants uniform, suiting up for two games. Initially, the Army didn't want to accept him due to their size limits, but he persuaded them to allow him to enlist. Blozis was a 250-pound tackle, but his size, nor the fact that he wasn't a quarterback, didn't prevent him from setting an Army hand grenade distance record when he heaved one for nearly 95 yards.

A few more nicknames: The 5'5" wide receiver Noland Smith was called "Super Gnat," there was a Clyde "Smackover" Scott, a "Turkey" Joe Jones, and Alan "The Horse" Ameche. Then there's Chad "Ocho Cinco" Johnson, who got his nickname because he wore jersey number 85, and the numerals 8 and 5 in Spanish are ocho and cinco. For a time he had his name legally changed to Ochocinco.

WHO WAS CALLED THE DIRTIEST PLAYER TO EVER APPEAR ON AN NFL FOOTBALL FIELD?

Although he's a forgotten player from long ago, a linebacker by the name of Hardy Brown proudly bore the nickname of "the Dirtiest Man in Pro Football." From 1948, his rookie season with the Brooklyn Dodgers of the AAFC, through 1960, this 6-foot, 190-pounder specialized in dishing out concussions and broken bones, often targeting jaws and cheekbones. Opposing running backs confessed they worried about him so much they avoided him, and they made certain to know where he was on the field at all times.

It may be an apocryphal story, but it's been said that one of his hits made such an impact on a ball-carrier that one of his eyeballs popped out of the socket and dangled down on his cheek, tenuously hanging on. It has also been reported that he knocked out around 80 opponents—knowing him, he may have decked a few teammates, officials, and cheerleaders, too.

Actually, over the years there have been numerous violent, though in some time periods legal tactics employed, from the head slap, to the leg whip, to the crackback block, and the clothesline tackle. *And* there have been quite a few players willing to deploy those tactics.

Two quick examples of proponents of rough, tough play, though, again, not necessarily dirty: Charley Taylor played most of his Hall of Fame career as a receiver, and he gained the reputation as one of the best blockers around. A Washington teammate of his, Bill Malinchak, noted, "He was probably the finest crack back blocker in football. He was one of the guys who probably led to the change of rules because he would come back on guys and lay them out. I mean he was deadly on these safeties. It was always a safety he seemed to get.

"You could crack back high, low, head, legs, anywhere at that time—it didn't matter. He was a big, strong guy, and quick. You'd get his whole body, it wasn't just his upper body hitting you. He would explode from the ground up . . . he would block through you." Opponents quickly learned to keep their head on a swivel when Taylor was around. "He had that reputation," said Malinchak. "He made people pay attention."

Another Hall of Famer was Dick "Night Train" Lane, whose famous weapon, later banned, was the clothesline tackle. He often brought ball-carriers down by going after their head and neck areas. He did that so often, and he was so effective at his signature move, that it became known as the Night Train Necktie. He said that when he tackled people by their legs, they could fall forward for extra yardage, maybe gaining a first down. On the other hand, as he once told a Sun-Telegram reporter, "I grab them around the neck so I can go back to the bench and sit down." Regardless of his rugged reputation, he was no thug. When he retired in 1965, his 68 career interceptions placed him behind only one NFL player ever, Emlen Tunnell.

DIRTY PLAY WAS NOT LIMITED TO A FEW PLAYERS—WHO IS ANOTHER MAN WHO TYPIFIED THE MEAN AND OFTEN DIRTY TACTICS THAT WENT ON AT ONE TIME?

Baltimore Colt Hall of Fame defensive end Gino Marchetti (1952–1966 career) called one of the middle linebackers he played with, Bill Pellington, "probably the meanest guy that ever wore a uniform, and he was my best friend. If receivers ran a crossing pattern, they'd go five yards out of the way *not* to go near him because he had the sharp elbows and he'd lay them out. And what made him a little meaner, he'd do it in practice. The guys would complain about it and he'd [dismiss them], 'Listen, they're going to do that to you in a game, so don't worry about it.'"

When Pellington had a broken arm, he continued to play, with a cast on his broken arm covered by tape. Marchetti recalled, "The referees checked it, but during halftime he'd take the tape off so that the cast was harder on opponents' heads."

In one game versus the Lions, Pellington's job was to slow their tight end from being able to get free downfield so "he was beating the hell out of him with his cast. The tight end went to the referee, complaining and complaining, and he finally said, 'Goddamnit, why the hell don't you just give him a gun?' The referee checked Bill, and he had that little extra strength there, taped up underneath his jersey. He had something that would give people a chance to worry. The referees always checked him, but somehow he hid it."

When it came to crazy, wild, and ferocious play, Marchetti was of the belief that linebackers reigned supreme. He felt nearly every linebacker was wild during his era. "They're crazy, no doubt about it. I think Joe Schmidt was the only one who had good sense."

TOUGHNESS IS A QUALITY USUALLY ASSOCIATED WITH POSITIONS SUCH AS MIDDLE LINEBACKER, AND THERE'S NO QUESTION THAT MEN SUCH AS DICK BUTKUS WERE AMONG THE TOUGHEST TO EVER SUIT UP IN THE NFL. BUT WHO STANDS OUT AS AN EXTREMELY TOUGH QUARTERBACK?

There have been some tough ones over the years such as the previously mentioned Bobby Layne, but another example who sharply stands out is Johnny Unitas. In Raymond Berry's autobiography *All the Moves I Had*, the Hall of Fame receiver who caught many a throw from Johnny U wrote, "We played the Bears twice a year in our division. They were 'The Monsters of the Midway' and it didn't make any difference what kind of monsters they were, John Unitas was not able to be intimidated. They'd hit him in the mouth and he just spit out his teeth, and he'd go back and beat you.

"We were playing them one time and somebody, a defensive lineman, came in and hit him right in the mouth and busted his nose. He didn't call time out because his nose was bleeding. What he did there on the field was he picked up some dirt [or mud], stuffed it up in his nose, got the blood stopped, and stepped back in the huddle—threw a touchdown pass. That's Unitas."

One opponent said Unitas got hit frequently because, being fearless, he'd hang in the pocket for an eon, until the very last second, looking for an open man. He contended that at times Unitas would purposely hold on to the football a bit longer than he had to before releasing it. He speculated that Unitas did that so he could take a lick then, looking at the tackler, laugh it off as if to say, "You can't hurt or unnerve me."

As a matter of fact, Miami Dolphins lineman Manny Fernandez said Unitas was one of the toughest quarterbacks he ever went up against. "You could just about break [his] ribs hitting them and they'd just get up, look at you, and say, 'Nice tackle.'" Plus, the first time Fernandez's Dolphins played against Unitas, the quarterback was 37 years old, but far from being a geriatric case.

WHAT FOOTBALL LEAGUES TRIED TO COMPETE WITH THE NFL IN AN ATTEMPT TO GAIN A FOOTHOLD ON THE AMERICAN PUBLIC, BUT FAILED?

The WFL (World Football League) was formed in 1973, had its first season in 1974, then folded before they could complete the following season. The main man behind the WFL was Gary Davidson, who was also in on the ground floor of the American Basketball Association and the World Hockey Association. Those leagues wound up having some teams join the established pro basketball and hockey leagues. The WFL wasn't as successful.

They did, however, steal some big talent from the NFL including three huge name Miami Dolphin players, Jim Kiick, Larry Csonka, and Paul Warfield in one swoop. That deal marked the most lucrative three-player deal in sports history to that point, at $3.5 million for what would turn out to be the doomed 1975 season.

One interesting facet of the WFL was its teams' nicknames, with so many of them being not plural words such as the Bears, but singular such as: Chicago Fire, Philadelphia Bell, Portland Storm and Portland Thunder, Southern California Sun, Jacksonville Express, and Shreveport Steamer.

The USFL (United States Football League) lived, but often on life support, for just three years. One reason the USFL was a fiasco was because the league, as bleacherreport.com put it, ". . . had a plan, failed to follow that plan, and let arrogance, new brash millionaire owners, weak central leadership, and the NFL itself beat it into submission."

At first, 12 cities, including eight which already hosted an NFL team, opened the 1983 USFL season, playing a spring/summer schedule. The league had a TV deal and wound up averaging 25,041 spectators per game. So far, so good.

However, two of the brash millionaire owners mentioned, Donald Trump and Eddie Einhorn, persuaded team owners to change to a fall schedule which then put the USFL in a head-butting contest with the mighty NFL. In short, teams began to lose money and fold, and the USFL sued the NFL. The jury's verdict was that the NFL had violated an antitrust law, but they dismissed eight other charges and determined the damage to the USFL was worthy of an award of one dollar.

Earlier, Trump tried to give his New York Generals more credibility by trying to lure Miami Dolphins coach Don Shula to guide his team. In 1983, the two reportedly were working on an agreement privately, and a contract signing looked favorable at first. Shula was offered a bump in his then $400,000 per year contract to a record-high coaching deal of $1 million per season.

Before the deal could be consummated, Trump went public with news about the high-profile coach (very prematurely thought Shula), appearing on TV during the halftime of a Miami game. Trump stated Shula was all set to sign a contract if his requests were met such as being provided with an apartment in Trump Tower. Shula, as one of his star players who was then a USFL team executive put it, was very upset that he had been "thrown out to the press" by Trump. Upset by the distraction of Trump's words, Shula announced that he was no longer interested in the Generals job.

DONALD TRUMP, OWNER OF THE USFL'S NEW JERSEY GENERALS, LAUNCHED AN ANTITRUST LAWSUIT AGAINST THE NFL.
(Wikimedia Commons)

Yet another rogue league formed then folded in one year when the XFL played its only season in 2001. Eight teams, all owned by the league and not individual owners, competed as a "joint venture between the World Wrestling Foundation and

NBC." The season began right after the NFL season concluded and it "featured sports entertainment elements inspired by professional wrestling," and that included "suggestively-dressed cheerleaders" and WWF men like Jesse Ventura doing commentary.

The XFL employed other changes in NFL rules or, as some said, they added gimmicks to the game such as the use of a black football with a red letter "X" on the sides of the ball. Players were permitted to use nicknames rather than their last names on their jerseys, and some changed their nickname on a weekly basis. Running back Rod Smart appeared in the XFL's first nationally televised game and gained instant recognition for sporting the nickname "He Hate Me" on the back of his jersey.

Also, instead of a coin toss determining who would gain initial possession of the ball, a player from each team was chosen to take part in a sprint from a 30 yard line to the football which rested on the 50 yard line. The winner of the dash was given the same choices as the winner of the opening coin toss in NFL games. In addition, no kicks after touchdowns were permitted—teams had to run a play from 2 yards out in order to score a single point after.

Nothing worked and the two organizations behind the league lost $35 million, causing NBC to cut ties with the XFL.

Then there was a league which purists believe deserves little, if any, attention—the Legends Football League, also known once as the Lingerie Football League. That organization was introduced at halftime of the Super Bowl in 2004. The first event, a pay-for-view game called the Lingerie Bowl, featured, what else—women playing football with padding, helmets, and, well, very little else. The league's first real season came in 2009, and there was little doubt about what they were selling—teams' names included the Las Vegas Sin, Los Angeles Temptation, Orlando Fantasy, Dallas Desire, Chicago Bliss, and the San Diego Seduction.

WHICH COACH HOLDS A RECORD FOR WINNING HIS DIVISION THE MOST CONSECUTIVE SEASONS?

Through 2020, New England's Bill Belichick, who also was the head coach at Cleveland (where he never won a division title), holds this mark. His Patriots headed their division for 11 straight seasons from 2009 through 2019. That's far ahead of the next group of coaches who won six division championships in a row: Chuck Noll with the Steelers, Bud Grant for the Vikings, Tom Landry of the Cowboys, and Cleveland's Paul Brown.

Belichick has also won the most postseason games in NFL history with 31, trailed by Landry's 20 and Don Shula's 19. Furthermore, counting pre–Super Bowl championships, Belichick is tied with two other coaches for the most championships ever won, six. The other men are George Halas and Curly Lambeau, with three of his titles from 1929 through 1931 coming in the days before championships were determined by playoffs.

WHO ARE THE THREE YOUNGEST MEN TO BE DRAFTED INTO THE NFL?

Because most players drafted by an NFL team are coming off the senior year of their college careers, the average age of drafted players is right around 22. The youngest man ever, though, was only 19.

Highly touted defensive tackle Amobi Okoye was selected by the Houston Texans in the first round as the 10th overall pick in the 2007 NFL Draft. He had moved from his native land of Nigeria to Alabama, and he graduated from high school when he was only 16 years old. He was accepted to attend Harvard University, but decided to play football for the University of Louisville, becoming the youngest man ever to play college football. When he appeared in his first professional game on September 9, 2007, he also became the youngest person ever to see action in an NFL contest.

The second-youngest man to make it to the NFL was defensive end Danielle Hunter, who began and finished his Louisiana State University college days early. Drafted by the Vikings in 2015, he soon became quite proficient when it comes to sacking quarterbacks.

The third-youngest player in an NFL game was another first-round pick, Tremaine Edmunds of the Buffalo Bills. He played two years for Virginia Tech before giving up his final years of eligibility. He not only was one of the youngest men to play in the NFL, he was the youngest man ever to pick off a pass. Still active in 2021, the linebacker who was drafted at the age of 20 in 2007 had gone to two Pro Bowls.

WHO ARE THE OLDEST MEN TO BE DRAFTED BY AN NFL TEAM?

Counting down from the third-oldest to the oldest player, the geriatric cases are Brandon Weeden, Chris Weinke, and Ove Johansson. All three were nearing their 30th birthday when drafted.

Despite his age, Weeden was a first-round pick in 2008, and that made him the oldest man ever to go in the first round. He got such a late start because he spent five years as a pitcher, playing for the New York Yankees and Los Angeles Dodgers organizations from 2002, when he was 18 years old, through 2006. In fact, in baseball, as in football, he was a first-round selection, but that sport, it turned out, wasn't for him—he went 19-26 with an inflated 5.02 ERA, and never made it as high as the Double-A level. So, turning to football, he played quarterback for Oklahoma State from 2008 through 2011, completing 69.5 percent of his passes.

Next comes Weinke, who wasn't picked until the sixth round of the NFL Draft in 2001. He also had seen some action in the minor leagues, but like Weeden, football was his stronger suit. As a matter of fact, he remains the oldest player ever to win the Heisman Trophy. However, his NFL days as a quarterback weren't as bright as his college days. He did hang around the NFL from 2001 through 2007, when he was 35 years old, but he started only 20 NFL games, losing 18, including one stretch in which his record as a starting quarterback was 0-17.

Finally, Johansson, a 5'10", 175-pound placekicker who was the Oilers' 12th-round pick, 316th overall selection, in 1977 when he was 29. The Swedish-born Johansson never saw his 30th birthday as an NFL player, lasting just two games, both with the Philadelphia Eagles. His NFL kicking log includes three attempted field goals, all from between 30 and 39 yards out, another failed kick of less than 20 yards, one successful field goal, and one extra point made out of three tries.

Johansson had only played college ball one year, hurting his knee in a bowl game in his college team's final game. Yet this is the same man mentioned earlier, famous for kicking the longest field goal in the history of organized football.

WHO WAS THE OLDEST MAN TO ACTUALLY PLAY AT LEAST ONE GAME IN THE NFL?

It was George Blanda, NFL's version of Methuselah, and he sure played in more than one game. He was able to last 26 seasons as a quarterback and placekicker, meaning his career spanned four different decades, a rarity. When he retired in 1975, he wasn't too far removed from turning 50—he was one week shy of his 49th birthday when his official retirement was announced.

He earned his pay all through the years. Upon his retirement he was the NFL's all-time leading scorer with 2,002 points scored, and that still holds down the number seven spot for a career. Almost exactly 6 percent of his lifetime throws went for scores, representing the 16th-best percentage to this day.

By the end of the 1970 season, Blanda owned or shared 37 professional football records, including firing 36 touchdowns in a season and his seven touchdowns thrown in a single game—and he still had five seasons left to play.

Blanda goes back so far that on the day he was born in 1927, Babe Ruth was well on his way to setting the single-season home run record with 60, and the NFL was only in its sixth season. Author Allan Maki quipped that when Blanda was inducted into the Hall at the age of 54, "he probably had another season or two left in him."

AT AGE 43 TOM BRADY WAS THE OLDEST STARTING QUARTERBACK TO WIN A SUPER BOWL. (Keith Allison via Wikimedia Commons)

Among players who were active at the start of the 2021 season, the distinction of being the oldest player is also, many say, the greatest player ever, Tom Brady. That despite the fact that in the 2000 Draft 198 players were chosen ahead of him.

Defying all odds, he showed no signs of slowing down at the age of 44. In fact, the 2021 season was one of his finest of his 22 years in the league. He led the league in passes attempted (719, 82 more than his next highest total); completions (485, his highest amount ever); yards gained on passes (5,316, his best total ever and the second time he went beyond the 5,000-yard mark); and touchdowns (43, his highest total ever and a new Tampa Bay record). He even led the NFL with his 312.7 yards through the air per game played which was his second best output ever. His completion rate of 67.5 in 2021 was his second highest percentage ever. Slowing down? Hardly—his quarterback rating in 2021 was 102.1, 4.5 points higher than his lifetime rating.

Behind Brady on the list of oldest players who were still active during the 2021 NFL season were offensive tackles Andrew Whitworth and Jason Peters; quarterbacks Ben Roethlisberger and Ryan Fitzpatrick; and punters Andy Lee and Sam Koch. (Roethlisberger and Whitworth retired following the 2021 season.)

Five of the seven oldest men on that list of the NFL's most robust survivors are punters or quarterbacks, and two long snappers whose careers ended in 2020 lasted until they were 39 years old, Don Muhlbach and L. P. Ladouceur.

WHO ARE SOME OF THE FOOTBALL PLAYERS WHO JUST HAPPENED TO BE BORN WITH NAMES WHICH ABSOLUTELY SOUND LIKE THESE MEN WERE DESTINED TO BE FEARSOME FOOTBALL PLAYERS? AND, WHO ARE SOME OF THE PLAYERS WHO EARNED NICKNAMES WHICH POINTED OUT JUST HOW TOUGH AND/OR FIERCE THEY WERE?

A few men with surnames which seemed to broadcast, "Don't mess with me," include legendary linebackers Dick Butkus and Ray Nitschke, superlative tight end Mike Ditka, defensive back Karl Kassulke, Andy Robustelli who was a Hall of Fame defensive end, and fellow Hall of Famer and bruising fullback Larry Csonka. The best three names well suited to the sport may well be Steve Stonebraker, who played tight end and linebacker, wide receiver Brian Baschnagel (pronounced BASH nay gull), and, from the Canadian Football League, linebacker/defensive end Steve Smear.

As for the players who earned nicknames with savage or fear-inspiring connotations, try a few of these on for size: Johnny "Blood" McNally, tackle Frank "Bruiser" Kinard, Sherman "Tank" Plunkett (another tackle, not as one might expect, a fullback), and linebacker Jack "Hacksaw" Reynolds who earned his nickname by once taking out his frustration over his Tennessee Volunteers disappointing defeat by taking a hacksaw to a car and actually cutting it in half. Then there were men such as defensive back Fred "The Hammer" Williamson, defensive tackle "Mean Joe" Greene, Bronko Nagurski, a fullback/linebacker/tackle with Ukrainian roots whose real first name was Bronislau, and Albert "Turk" Edwards, yet another tackle, who is now a long forgotten player, but a member of the Hall of Fame.

ON THE OTHER HAND, WHO HAD NAMES WHICH DIDN'T SOUND AT ALL RUGGED?

Proving the line from *Romeo and Juliet* about what's in a name, many NFL players including some greats had names which may have caused them to get teased, but probably not by those who knew better than to mess around with strong and sturdy football players. Take Hall of Famer Bob Lilly of the Dallas Cowboys—few people wanted to tangle with this 6'5", 260-pound defensive lineman. Another player with a flower-like name was Rosey (Roosevelt) Grier. He also had his position and size as a common point with Lilly. Grier went 6'5" and weighed in at 284 pounds. After his playing days were over, he became, among other things, a bodyguard for Senator Robert Kennedy, and he was guarding Kennedy's wife Ethel when Kennedy was assassinated.

A few other examples of not-so-tough names include Elvis Peacock, Paddy Driscoll, Milt Plum, and three players with "shy" in their names—brothers Don and Les Shy, both running backs in the late 1960s and a bit into the 1970s, and the 300-pound Shyheim (who went by Shy) Tuttle.

Some players even had names which may not have had the most pleasant of connotations, but that didn't hold them back. Defensive lineman Jethro Pugh (pronounced pew as in cartoon character Pepe Le Pew) had a long and productive career, twice being on Super Bowl winning Dallas Cowboy teams. Finally, running back Elijah Pitts of the Green Bay Packers is one of 10 men to make it to the NFL with that surname, including recent players Lafayette, Kyle, and Chester.

WHO ARE SOME OF THE COACHES WHO HAVE ACHIEVED SUCCESS IN BOTH THE COLLEGE RANKS AND THE NFL?

Well, Jimmy Johnson is certainly one. He is in the Pro Football Hall of Fame after coaching Dallas and the Miami Dolphins and winning 144 games, plus his winning back-to-back Super Bowl titles for the 1992 and 1993 seasons. He also won close to 70 percent of the NFL games he coached in postseason play.

Johnson is the first of just two coaches to win a Super Bowl and an NCAA championship, achieving that at the University of Miami in 1987 where his record over a five-year span was 52-9. For that, and his many other accomplishments, he was voted into the College Football Hall of Fame. Trivia note: One of Johnson's high school classmates was singer Janis Joplin.

Coincidentally, the other coach to win it all at the college and pro levels was Barry Switzer, who wound up replacing Johnson as the head coach of the Cowboys. In addition, Switzer was a coach on the staff of the University of Arkansas where both Cowboys owner Jerry Jones and Johnson played their college ball as offensive linemen, and where they won the National Championship for the 1964 season.

Switzer won the Super Bowl in just his second season as the Cowboys head man, in 1995. His records over his first three of four seasons in the NFL were: 12-4, 12-4, and 10-6. Previously, over a college coaching career which lasted for 16 seasons, all leading the Oklahoma Sooners, his winning percentage was a lofty .837 based on 157 victories versus just 29 defeats and four ties. He won National Championships in 1974, 1975, and 1985.

WHO ARE THE COACHES WHO HAVE WON BACK-TO-BACK SUPER BOWL TITLES? RELATED QUESTION: WHICH COACH ACTUALLY WON THE NFL TITLE THREE YEARS IN A ROW, WITH ONE OF HIS CHAMPIONSHIPS COMING PRIOR TO THE INCEPTION OF THE SUPER BOWL?

Through the 2020 season, six men have managed back-to-back Super Bowl victories: the previously mentioned Johnson, Bill Belichick, Mike Shanahan with the Denver Broncos, Chuck Noll who did this twice, Don Shula with the Miami Dolphins, including the only perfect season (17-0) in 1972, and Vince Lombardi with the Green Bay Packers.

As for winning three championships in successive seasons, one man stands out, Lombardi. He won the 1966 NFL title and followed that up by winning the first two Super Bowls. No other coach has ever strung together three consecutive NFL championships. To top things off, Lombardi wound up winning five NFL titles over a seven-year timeframe.

WHO ARE THE COACHES WHO HAVE LOST FOUR SUPER BOWLS?

Bud Grant of the Minnesota Vikings was the first coach to do this. He made it to four of the first 11 Super Bowls but came home empty-handed each time. As great a coach as Don Shula was, he also came up short on four occasions. Buffalo head coach Marv Levy's plight is an even sadder tale than that of Grant and Shula as his Super Bowl losses all came in a row. Dan Reeves lost all four of the Super Bowls he coached in for Denver and Atlanta, once making it to the championship game three times over a four-year period.

Unfortunately, Reeves still has the sad distinction of being the coach of the losing team in the most lopsided defeat in Super Bowl history when his Broncos fell to San Francisco, 55–10, in 1990. Despite his numerous division and conference titles, his nine trips to the Super Bowl as a player, assistant coach, and head coach, and in spite of his 190 career wins, he has yet to gain Hall of Fame status. Reeves even has the most career wins of any coach who is not in the Hall with the exception of Marty Schottenheimer, who notched 200 victories.

Acknowledgments

I'd like to acknowledge Niels Aaboe, senior acquisitions editor for Globe Pequot/Lyons Press, who came up with the idea to do a book which would explain the whys and wherefores of the game of football.

I also appreciate the very interesting insights of my cousin Dale Stewart, who played service and college football. Thanks also to the many NFL players who were gracious enough to sit through interviews with me—men such as Raymond Berry, Mike Ditka, Mike Lucci, Fred Cox, Dave Robinson, Joe Walton, Lenny Moore, Bill Malinchak, Sam Havrilak, Myron Pottios, Doug Crusan, Jackie Smith, Floyd Little, Gino Marchetti, Andy Nelson, Manny Fernandez, Mel Renfro, Rick Volk, Tom Matte, Paul Warfield, and other people affiliated with football such as Bill Keenist of the Detroit Lions front office, Jon Kendle of the Pro Football Hall of Fame, and West Virginia University star Chuck Smith.

Thanks also to my sons, Sean and Scott Stewart, as well as my grandson, Nathan Stewart, for their input/help in researching this book.

Finally, a note about two of the sources I relied upon heavily. Without two outstanding websites, that of the Pro Football Hall of Fame and Pro Football Reference, this book would have been immensely more difficult to write. Being able to explore and depend upon those sources (and others) made the book a joy to write.

Sources

Books

Some of the material used in this book comes from previous books the author has written on football:

All the Moves I Had: A Football Life (with Raymond Berry). Guilford, CT: Lyons Press, 2016.

America's Football Factory: Western Pennsylvania's Cradle of Quarterbacks from Johnny Unitas to Joe Montana. Kent, OH: Kent State University Press/Black Squirrel Books, 2018.

Remembering the Greatest Coaches and Games of the NFL Glory Years: An Inside Look at the Golden Age of Football. Lanham, MD: Rowman & Littlefield, 2018.

Remembering the Stars of the NFL Glory Years: An Inside Look at the Golden Age of Football. Lanham, MD: Rowman & Littlefield, 2017.

You're the Ref: 174 Scenarios to Test Your Football Knowledge. New York: Skyhorse Publishing, 2015.

Additional Books Used

Dorsett, Tony, and Harvey Frommer. *Running Tough: Memoirs of a Football Maverick.* New York: Doubleday, 1989.

MacCambridge, Michael, ed. *ESPN College Football Encyclopedia.* New York: ESPN, 2005.

Whittingham, Richard. *Sunday's Heroes: NFL Legends Talk About the Times of Their Lives.* Chicago: Triumph Books, 2003.

Websites

www.athlonsports.com

www.baltimoresun.com

www.bleacherreport.com

www.businessinsider.com

www.chicago.sbnation.com

www.constructiondive.com

www.deseret.com

www.edge.twinspires.com

www.en.as.com

www.espn.com

www.fanbuzz.com

www.footballiqscore.com

www.foxsports.com

www.gallaudetathletics.com

www.history.com

www.heisman.com

www.ideas.time.com

www.kansascity.com

www.krauskollc.com

www.medium.com

www.miamidolphins.com

www.nbcsports.com

www.newenglandhistoricalsociety.com

www.ozy.com

www.pff.com

www.profootballhof.com

www.pro-football-reference.com

www.profootballtalk.nbcsports.com

www.psychologytoday.com

www.sbnation.com

www.si.com

www.smithsonianmag.com
www.sportingnews.com
www.sportscasting.com
www.statista.com
www.texaslsn.org
www.thebigredzone.com
www.theguardian.com
www.theversed.com
www.tiebreaker.com
www.turnonthejets.com
www.washingtonpost.com
www.yardbreaker.com

About the Author

Wayne Stewart was born and raised in Donora, Pennsylvania, a town that has produced several big-league baseball players, including Stan Musial and the father-son Griffeys. Stewart now lives in Amherst, Ohio, and is married to Nancy (Panich) Stewart.

He has covered the sports world as a writer for more than 40 years, beginning in 1978. He has interviewed and profiled many stars including Kareem Abdul-Jabbar and Larry Bird as well as numerous baseball legends such as Nolan Ryan, Bob Gibson, Tony Gwynn, Greg Maddux, Rickey Henderson, and Ken Griffey Jr.

In addition, Stewart has written more than 20 baseball books and a handful of other books on football and basketball. His works have also appeared in seven baseball anthologies. This is his 37th book.

Stewart has also written over 500 articles for publications such as *Baseball Digest*, *USA Today/Baseball Weekly*, *Boys' Life*, and Beckett Publications and has written for the official publications of many Major League Baseball teams including the Braves, Yankees, White Sox, Orioles, Padres, Twins, Phillies, Red Sox, A's, and Dodgers.

Furthermore, Stewart has appeared, as a baseball expert/historian, on Cleveland's Fox 8, on an ESPN Classic television show on Bob Feller, and on numerous radio shows. He also hosted his own radio shows including a call-in sports talk show, a pregame Indians report, and pregame shows for Notre Dame football.